THE QUESTION OF GOVERNMENT SPENDING

THE QUESTION OF GOVERNMENT SPENDING

Public Needs and Private Wants

FRANCIS M. BATOR

HARPER & BROTHERS PUBLISHERS NEW YORK

THE QUESTION OF GOVERNMENT SPENDING

Printed in the United States of America

Library of Congress catalog card number: 6-7556

To My Father

CONTENTS

CONTENTS

TABLES

. . . The ideas of economists and political philosophers, both when they are right and when they are wrong, are more powerful than is commonly understood. Indeed the world is ruled by little else. Practical men, who believe themselves to be quite exempt from any intellectual influences, are usually the slaves of some defunct economist. Madmen in authority, who hear voices in the air, are distilling their frenzy from some academic scribbler of a few years back. I am sure that the power of vested interests is vastly exaggerated compared with the gradual encroachment of ideas. Not, indeed, immediately, but after a certain interval; for in the field of economic and political philosophy there are not many who are influenced by new theories after they are twenty-five or thirty years of age, so that the ideas which civil servants and politicians and even agitators apply to current events are not likely to be the newest. But, soon or late, it is ideas, not vested interests, which are dangerous for good or evil.—JOHN MAYNARD KEYNES, *The General Theory of Employment, Interest, and Money,* Macmillan, 1936, p. 383.

PREFACE

> "Would you tell me, please, which way I ought to go from here?" [asked Alice].
> "That depends a good deal on where you want to get to," said the Cat.

THE contention of this book is that much of our public discussion of the past few years about government spending has been beside the point; that whatever the right answers may be, we have not asked, and have not been asked, the right questions. My plea is neither for less government spending, nor, strictly speaking, for more, but rather for clear thought about what is involved in the choice.

Nonetheless, the argument will not appear neutral. The main reason is that it casts doubt on some propositions about public spending which the opponents of such spending regard as central to their case. But though those propositions, as I hope to show, are wrong or irrelevant, it does not follow that people like myself who favor increasing the public share in output are necessarily right. In its logical implications the argument *is* neutral and not inconsistent with the view that we should reduce public spending. In a sense the book is designed not to provide answers but to instill uncertainty concerning matters about which many people are all too groundlessly certain.

Still, the overtones—the emphasis, the choice of examples—are not neutral, any more than is my motivation in addressing a book on complicated and technical matters not primarily to economists but to the persistent lay reader interested in public affairs. One's conception of what is a good society is inevitably subjective, and one's appraisal of the future uncertain. *My* conception of the good society, and my apprehension of the threats and the opportunities we confront, lead me to believe that we are dangerously shortchanging ourselves on defense, foreign aid, education, urban renewal, and medical services; that we badly need to increase allocations to these and a variety of other public tasks. And if I am concerned that we ask the right questions, and that we pay attention to the facts, it is no doubt partly because I am inclined to think that once the issues are clearly posed, more people than not will tend to agree.

FRANCIS M. BATOR

Cambridge, Massachusetts
November 1, 1959

ACKNOWLEDGMENTS

FOR help in my search for unpublished data I am indebted to Samuel Cohn of the Bureau of the Budget, George Jaszi of the Department of Commerce, David Lusher of the Council of Economic Advisers, and Walter Salant of the Brookings Institution. Mr. Cohn made available to me what were at that time (to my knowledge) the only estimates on the functional composition of federal purchases of goods and services. (The estimates had been prepared by Mr. Cohn, Mrs. Naomi Sweeney, and Mr. Charles Stockman.)

For research and computational assistance I am grateful to Phoebus Dhrymes, Arnold Saffer, and Richard Roseman. Messrs. Dhrymes and Saffer performed most of the computations and bore up nobly during many a statistical crisis.

For finance of research assistance and for clerical and editorial help I am indebted to Professor W. W. Rostow's American Project at the Center for International Studies and to the Department of Economics, M.I.T. I must thank also the John Simon Guggenheim Memorial Foundation. I did the work of converting a long chapter into a short book during the first three months of my tenure as a Guggenheim Fellow.

Of those who were good enough to read and comment on a previous draft, I must mention especially, Paul, Peter, and

Victor Bator, Donald Blackmer, Thomas Devine, Richard Hatch, Edwin Kuh, Lucian Pye, Arthur Singer, and Robert Solow. I am particularly grateful to Blackmer, Singer, and, most of all, to the Center for International Studies' beleaguered guardian of the king's English, Richard Hatch; they constituted a discerning and persistent jury of lay critics.

This book grew out of an invitation by Professor Ralph Freeman to contribute a chapter to his symposium *Postwar Economic Trends in the United States* (Harper, 1960). I am grateful to him for agreeing to separate publication.

Last, I should like to thank the director of the Center for International Studies, Max Millikan. My indebtedness to him will be appreciated by anyone who knows the Center.

THE QUESTION OF GOVERNMENT SPENDING

1 ON GOVERNMENT SPENDING

OUR postwar political history reflects an intense preoccupation with government spending, a pervasive sense that expenditure by government has been perilously high. Periodically, it is true, this sense of excess has been dulled by dramatic reminders of national crisis; the threat of a Communist Europe, a Communist-conquered Korea, and two Sputniks—these diverted us from our budgetary anxieties. But not for long. Reaction soon set in, leading, if not to less government spending, at least to firmer resistance against more.

A sequence of crisis-induced spending followed by retrenchment is not, in itself, surprising. People do not like taxes, and politicians like to win elections. What makes public concern over the budget worth noting is the persistence of a contrapuntal theme. Much of the best public thought on national affairs in the last ten or so years has had its origins in the deliberations of various public and private committees of disinterested and conservative men, always distinguished and often wise. And most of these, when charged with study of specific situations of public interest, have made recommendations which coincide in one important respect: they cost more money. In fact, there has been near-unanimity among people informed about the condition of particular areas in the province of government (school building, medical research, teachers' salaries, urban slums, air defense, and the like) that there is acute need for more public spending.

Nor, it is fair to say, has opposition to spending been supported by head-on rebuttal of the claims on behalf of schools—or missiles. It has been based, rather, on the supposed effects of increased spending on the "health" of the body politic. "Ruinous inflation," "stunting of growth," "bankruptcy," "depression (hair curling)" have been the slogans, frequently supplemented by invocation of the more subtle threat of "creeping socialism." On an extreme but not uncommon view, we have been on the verge of spending our way to national collapse—at least in the "long run." On a more moderate but more widely held view, if we have not yet crossed the line of danger, we have strayed uncomfortably close.

Superimposed, the two themes define a cruel dilemma. If we are to meet the "essential" demands of national security, let alone of decent education for our children and of the other requirements of a good society, we shall, it appears, have to suffer great economic and social damage. Or shall we? At the least, is it not paradoxical that a country of unmatched material riches, the world's one "affluent society," should be faced by such a painful choice?

The question of what level of government spending is tolerable, of what we can and should afford, cannot, in the end, be resolved by recourse to fact or logic. The answer will be, must be, sensitive to *values:* values as to the allocation and distribution of material resources, and, perhaps more important, as to modes of social and political organization. But if we are to do our best by *some* set of values, our choices must be based on clear understanding of the consequences of feasible alternatives; and identification of what is feasible, as of consequences, is very much a matter of fact and analysis. Indeed, disagreement over values makes careful analysis the more important—it can narrow the area of controversy to what is really irreconcilable, and thereby expose any illusory dilemmas. To do so with regard to certain aspects of public spending is the purpose of this book.

It is appropriate to begin with some quantitative history. What has been the rate of public spending for various purposes? Federal spending? State and local spending? What fraction of the economy's output has such spending diverted to government use? Part One presents the essential facts, year by year, since 1929. Public spending (total and per capita) is broken down by source and by major function (defense, education, road building, etc.) with differentiation throughout between purchases of goods and services and "nonexhaustive" spending, so called, such as unemployment compensation, old-age pensions, and the like. Calculations are also made of the public share in constant (1957) prices, to eliminate the fictitious effects due to price inflation; of the relation of the various "nondefense" components of public purchases to nondefense output; of the volume of public capital formation; and of how the share of government in the United States compares with that in some other countries.

Part Two—the greater part of the book—is an attempt to sort out some of the tangled issues of interpretation and value which have shaped the postwar debate on what we can afford, with particular attention to the more popular rules frequently advanced to guide spending policy. It examines whether the goal of avoiding inflation is a sufficient or even useful guide to the proper level of public spending. It tests the two-pronged claim that any substitution of political for private market choice through increased public spending will, in general, "worsen" the allocation of resources and that, in fact, government spending in the postwar period has been the cause of gross misallocation. The crucial questions are two: (1) Has the share of government in total output forced us to skimp, in terms of widely held values, on consumption and private investment? What are the facts on which one would have to base a presumption that we have so skimped? (2) Apart from any skimping, what does the scale of public spending imply about the efficiency of the economy in catering to consumers' wants? Has government spending caused us to violate the principle of "consumer sovereignty"? The book concludes with some comments on government spending in relation to the grand issues of coercion and freedom.

Before proceeding, a double note of caution is in order. (1) The purpose of what follows is to examine some of the much debated implications of government spending. Such spending must not be confused with government production. It is, in concept, entirely possible for the government of a fully socialist country to carry on with a very small budget of purchases of goods and services, though all means of production be owned and operated by the state—for example, if all final production by public enterprise is for sale to private buyers, with civil servant managers under orders either to show a profit or to go out of business. Alternatively, government could purchase the whole national product, though all production be in private hands. There is no necessary connection. (2) As the above implies, the book is not designed to assess the total economic impact of government. Many powerful devices in the public armory besides nationalization are only trivially dependent on spending (e.g., regulation of security issues, of public utilities, of food-labeling; antitrust). In fact, it is only recently that spending has displaced questions of regulation and control, of institutional reform, as the most chewed-over bone of contention. But here attention is on spending.[1]

[1] Even if one is interested in spending, one cannot ignore all other means of control. It is obvious, for instance, that an evaluation of the consequences of spending for, say, income distribution requires attention to, e.g., taxation. Moreover, a number of instruments of control are partial substitutes for government spending. But here I treat other instruments only as these appear relevant to an assessment of the effects of spending.

Part One

FACTS

2 SOME QUANTITATIVE HISTORY (1)

"Nonexhaustive" Expenditure

SIMPLY to add up all the money paid out each year by public agencies as recorded in their accounts is not a very revealing exercise. Not all spending is alike; to derive insight from expenditure figures one must distinguish, at the least, between two kinds: "exhaustive" expenditure (G) and "nonexhaustive" expenditure (N).

"Exhaustive" expenditure, so called, is spending that "absorbs" goods and services. It consists of *purchases* by government of goods and services from business and households (e.g., of typewriters and B-52's, and of the services of construction companies and of civil servants). Its total is a measure of the net claim of government on current production and hence of the volume of output not available for personal consumption or private investment. It also measures the volume of production not subject to a "market test," i.e., to a purchase by a private buyer.

"Nonexhaustive" expenditure is spending that absorbs no output but redistributes income or assets. Made up of interest on the public debt, of such transfer payments as unemployment compensation, unrestricted cash grants to veterans, old-age and retirement benefits, and of federal grants-in-aid to state and local governments, nonexhaustive expenditure is best thought of as the obverse of taxes. Like taxes, it redistributes "dollar votes"; and unlike purchases of goods and services, it does not constitute a claim on labor or other scarce resources. It does not, as do, e.g., the wages of civil servants, represent payment for current services rendered. (The cost of administering programs of nonexhaustive expenditure is, of course, a part of purchases of goods and services.)[1]

Except for a brief look at the magnitude and composition of nonexhaustive expenditure (N), primary attention in what follows is on the first category, government purchases of goods and services (G). But it is well to emphasize that neither G nor indeed *total* public spending (E, i.e., G + N) should be thought of as that will-o'-the-wisp: a measure of the volume of resources the allocation of which is in some sense "determined" by government. Both exhaustive and nonexhaustive expenditure affect allocation: the first by directly bidding for resources, and both by altering the disposable incomes and asset-positions of individuals, business firms, and units of government. But so

[1] The distinction between exhaustive and nonexhaustive expenditure is not in all cases clear, even in concept. Moreover, the available statistical information does not always fit the categories even where there is no intrinsic ambiguity. How, for instance, is one to treat government enterprises which produce for sale to private buyers? While it is the burden of "net" in "net resource-absorbing expenditure" that one must not count in their expensable purchases on current account (e.g., the expenses of a profitable municipal power plant), one cannot completely ignore such enterprises—they are not all profitable. Any publicly subsidized excess of expenses over sales revenue in running, say, post-offices or post-exchanges, or, for that matter, some private facility, implies government resource absorption. The amount of the subsidy, however, is a very poor measure of such "absorption" and hence I shall follow the Commerce Department practice of excluding "subsidies less current surplus of government enterprises" from exhaustive expenditure. Where such exclusion makes a significant quantitative difference, footnotes contain alternative calculations combining "subsidies less surplus" and purchases of goods and services. (For discussion of some other ambiguities, see notes on pp. 24 and 37.)

do a host of other governmental measures which entail no public spending or lending, such as the licensing of broadcast bands, tariffs, policing of airplane safety, and the like. Anything that affects the profitability of some activity or the composition of private spending, whether directly, as do taxes, or more indirectly by altering the pattern of prices or availabilities (of, say, mortgage money or sugar), will have more or less pervasive effects on supply and demand throughout the economy.[2]

On the other hand, it is G and not the *total* of public spending (E) which measures the volume of resources "absorbed" by government; to use the ratio of total government spending to gross national product, E/GNP, as an indicator of the public claim on output, as is frequently done, is most misleading. The nonexhaustive components of spending do not constitute such a claim; it would be possible for the ratio to exceed 100 per cent, though the government was absorbing only a fraction of GNP, with private consumption and investment taking the rest.

Nonexhaustive Expenditure (N)[3]

What has been the history since 1929 of all-government, federal, and state-local nonexhaustive spending? What are the

[2] To think sensibly about the question of how many dollars' worth of output are "influenced" by government purchases, one should think about it in the way one would think about an urn filled with marbles. How many of ninety black marbles in an urn containing a hundred marbles have their positions influenced by the ten white marbles? The relationships are likely to exhibit mutual interdependence. The resource-composition of personal consumption is as much a cause as a consequence of the resource-composition of the government's share in output.

[3] To economize on space I make liberal use in all that follows of the symbols G (for all-government exhaustive expenditure) and N (for all-government nonexhaustive expenditure). Some use is made also of FG and FN, to represent federal exhaustive and nonexhaustive spending; and of SG and SN for the corresponding state-local magnitudes. GNP stands for gross national product and E (used only a few times) for

interesting trends? Tables 1 and 2 contain the basic data: the amount and composition, year by year, of nonexhaustive expenditure (N), as well as the statistics on exhaustive expenditure (G) and on total expenditure (E).[4]

The most striking thing about the series on all-government nonexhaustive spending is the tremendous increase between 1929 and 1957. N grew fifteenfold (from under $1.7 billion per annum to $25.5 billion in 1957) as compared with a tenfold increase in purchases of goods and services (G), a somewhat more than fourfold increase in gross national product, and a 40 per cent increase in population. Even if corrected for inflation-caused shrinkage in the dollar yardstick by say 85 per cent (using the price index for GNP), the rise in the annual volume of purchasing power subject to interpersonal transfer via government has been dramatic. In 1957, 23 per cent of public expenditure consisted of nonexhaustive spending, as compared with 17 per cent of a much smaller total in 1929.

What explains the fifteenfold rise in government nonexhaustive expenditure since 1929? It is evident from the composition of N that social security and World War II must take much of the blame—with an assist by the Korean War. Between 88-100 per cent of annual nonexhaustive spending since 1929 has consisted of *transfer payments* and of *interest on the*

---

total government spending, i.e., for G + N. [The reader not quantitatively inclined, who may well find the rest of this and the next chapter slow going, can read pp. 12-39 selectively without loss of continuity. Anyone interested only in the qualitative policy issues (and willing to miss some fascinating facts about the role of government in the United States) might just glance at the headings before turning to Part Two.]

[4] Except where otherwise indicated, the years 1947-1957 should be understood in all that follows to denote fiscal years, while years prior to 1947 refer to calendar years. I was forced to adopt this procedure because I was unable to convert the 1947-1957 data on the functional composition of government purchases to a calendar year basis yet needed comparable totals (cf. note 12, p. 29).

public debt, with transfers in 1957 taking 72 per cent (about par for the postwar decade) and interest 23 per cent. Of the interest, over four-fifths is attributable to the financing of World War II—i.e., about $5 billion of a 1957 total of $6 billion. And of the $18.4 billion of transfers that year, a fourth was accounted for by cash grants to veterans, and the other three-fourths by direct relief and by benefit payments from the various social insurance trust funds (e.g., old-age and survivors, unemployment, railroad retirement, federal civilian pensions). In 1957, then, a little more than half of all nonexhaustive spending reflected the cost of social security, and another third (plus) was a heritage of the war and of Korea.[5]

In view of the role of war finance and of the social security programs of New Deal vintage, it is not surprising that the lion's share of postwar nonexhaustive expenditure has been federal. In 1929 interest paid by state-local governments made up $.5 billion of a total government interest bill of $.9 billion; by 1957 the federal government paid $5.5 billion of the $6 billion total. (State-local interest payments, net of interest receipts, have shown no trend rise at all since 1929.) And of transfer spending since 1947, the federal government has been responsible for about three-fourths. In 1957, for instance, the federal component came to 80 per cent of the $18.4 billion total—about the same percentage as in 1929, when the federal share in transfers was 78 per cent (of a $.9 billion total). (During most years of the mid- and late 1930's, in contrast, the federal share fluctuated between a third and a half.)[6]

[5] The all-government interest bill (net) came to $.9(+) billion in 1929, $1.3 billion in 1941, $4.5 billion in 1946, remained under $5 billion until 1952, and then rose to $6 billion in 1957. The attribution of four-fifths of the 1957 amount to war finance is based on the rise in the net federal debt between 1940 and 1945 relative to the increase in net all-government debt between 1929 and 1957. For the data, see *Economic Report of the President,* Jan. 1959, p. 194.

[6] Federal net interest payments totaled $.4 billion in 1929, $.8 billion in 1941, $4.2 billion in 1947 (fiscal), and $5.5 billion in 1957. (*Cont'd.*)

Moreover, the above comparisons do not tell the whole story. An appreciable fraction of state-local transfers is financed by *federal* grants-in-aid to state and local governments. Rising from a 1929 level of $.1 billion to $1.5 billion in 1947 and $3.6 billion in 1957, such grants constitute an intra-governmental transaction; hence they do not show up in the net total of all-government nonexhaustive spending. But in the postwar period they have accounted for 10-15 per cent of the nonexhaustive expenditures of the federal government (with no trend)—percentages well below the 1933-1943 figures, but above the 1929 ratio of 9 per cent. (In calendar 1957, $1.3 billion of the $4.1 billion of federal grants to state and local governments went for highway and other transport; $1.8 billion for social security and welfare services—this helped finance state-local outlays of $2.9 billion; a little less than $.3 billion was used for education, and the rest to help finance miscellaneous other state and local activities.)[7]

Federal benefit payments from the various social insurance funds rose from $44 million in 1929 to a pre-1945 peak of $835 million in 1940, to $1.3 billion in 1945, approximately $2.2 billion in 1947 and 1948, up to $6.1 billion in calendar 1950 (due to the 1949 recession); went down to $4.4 billion in calendar 1951, up again to $5.6 billion in calendar 1953 and to $11.2 billion in the recession-ridden calendar year of 1957. The big increase in various veterans' disability and compensation payments—the second major category of federal transfers—followed World War II ($.5 billion in 1939, $6.9 billion in 1946, $4.3 billion in calendar 1951, and $4.7 billion in calendar 1957).

State and local transfers—these consist of two kinds of social insurance payments: government pensions and cash sickness compensation, and of direct relief—rose from $218 million in 1929 to $1.0 billion in 1937, $1.6 billion in 1946, and $4.0 billion in calendar 1957. In the postwar period relief payments have made up about two-thirds of the total.

[7] There is still another category of nonexhaustive expenditure—"subsidies less current surplus of government enterprises." (Subsidies consist of government payments to farmers, payments for the exportation and diversion of surplus agricultural commodities, shipping and housing subsidies, the wartime subsidy programs administered by the

A few additional facts about postwar trends in nonexhaustive expenditure might be noted:

While interest on the public debt continued to grow during the postwar decade (from $4.5 billion in 1946 to $6.0 billion in 1957), national income—the sum total of wages, salaries, professional and proprietors' incomes, profits and interest—grew even faster. In 1946, 2.47 per cent of the national income was subject to redistribution from taxpayers to holders of government bonds. By 1957 the ratio was down to 1.67 per cent, above the 1929 figure of 1.12 per cent, but not appreciably higher than in 1939 (1.66 per cent) and of course much lower than during the worst of the depression. The ratio of the *federal* component of interest to national income, in turn, while it tripled between 1929 and 1957, has fallen sharply since 1946, from 2.31 per cent to, e.g., 1.53 per cent in 1957.

What about transfer payments? For all governments taken together, transfers involved 6 per cent of national income in 1946 and 5.1 per cent in 1957. (The 1929 ratio was 1.04 per cent; that in 1939, 3.45 per cent.) In 1957 federal transfers alone came to 4.06 per cent of national income, as compared with 5.09 per cent in 1946. (In 1929, the ratio was .79 per cent.)

C.C.C. and the R.F.C., and subsidy payments to air carriers.) "Subsidies less surplus" would be particularly troublesome—subsidies do reflect some absorption of resources by government, i.e., a partial short circuit of private markets—were it not that in the postwar, until 1957 at least, the total did not amount to a significant proportion of N. Excluding 1957, the postwar average was negative; and 1956 and 1957 were the only postwar years during which the total came to more than $.3 billion (or more than 1.8 per cent of N). On the other hand, the total does hide more than it reveals. Surpluses realized by government enterprises generally offset the often sizable subsidies involved in the agricultural program. (In calendar 1957, agricultural subsidies alone ran to $2½ billion.) Moreover, federal subsidies-less-surpluses have generally been larger than the all-government total—the state-local figures have all been negative. (For the figures, see Table 2.)

To summarize: nonexhaustive expenditure, i.e., spending which does not constitute a claim on resources and does not short-circuit private market allocation of resources, has accounted for between one-sixth and one-third of total government spending since the war, with the ratio generally higher than in 1929 and much higher than during the war. N has been especially significant in the federal budget. The ratio of federal nonexhaustive expenditure to total federal spending has ranged between a quarter and a half during the last ten or so years, with social security, veterans' benefits, and interest on the government debt taking the lion's share. Again, none of these programs should be thought of as diverting substantial resources from private consumption or private capital formation. As will be argued below, the "economic" case for or against nonexhaustive expenditure must, in the first instance, hinge on ethical issues of income distribution.

3 SOME QUANTITATIVE HISTORY (2)

"Exhaustive" Expenditure

THE second category of public spending—government purchase of goods and services (G)—is quite another matter. It does divert resources from production for private account; indeed, it is the best measure of the volume of resources "absorbed" by government, of current production not submitted to the test of a sale to a private buyer. What has been its history since 1929?[1]

[1] For the "raw" statistics on all-government, federal, and state-local purchases of goods and services, see Columns 2, 5, and 8 of Table 1. (Recall that 1929-1946 stand for calendar years, and 1947-1957 for fiscal years. Fiscal 1957 was chosen as the terminal year because calendar 1957 and fiscal 1958 reflect the special circumstances of recession. We are concerned with the allocation of resources between private and public use in periods when resources are scarce and not when substantial resources are idle.)

In a conveniently tidy world, the total of government purchases would correspond more or less exactly to the volume of resources that would be available to increase the production of private consumer goods and services, and of capital goods on private account, *if* exhaustive public expenditure were kept to zero. In the disorderly world in which the national income statistician must do his work, this is not quite the case: some of the services of the government, e.g., road maintenance to truckers, are not "final" goods but intermediate to private production; they are, in effect, inputs required by producers to maintain the current level of their output for private use. Since we have no good measure

All-Government Totals

The rise in public purchases, G, though not of the same order as in nonexhaustive expenditure, is again imposing. In 1957, G was ten times what it had been in 1929—less than during the height of the war in 1943-1944, but three times its 1947 level. Some of the increase reflects inflation-caused shrinkage in the unit of measure; in "real" terms, G* (all "deflated" series will be marked by an asterisk) has also grown, but by a factor of four rather than ten. It increased by two-thirds during the 1930's, by a multiple of five between 1939 and 1944, then declined by 1947 to about one-and-a-quarter times its 1939 level only to double again between 1947 and 1957. (Chart 1 and Columns 1-3 of Table 3 contain the "deflated" figures, which measure exhaustive spending in terms of the 1957 price level.)

Of course G* is not the only thing that has increased since 1929. Population too has grown, as has total "real" output, GNP*. For perspective, it is well to look at G* per head of population, and at the ratio of public purchases to GNP. (See Columns 6-12 of Table 3 and also Chart 2.)

In terms of 1957 prices, government purchases of goods and services per head of population rose from $169 in 1929 to $498 in 1957, i.e., by a factor of three. Per capita "real" gross national product, in turn, increased about one-and-a-half times, from $1,587 to $2,545. The *share* of government purchases in total output during the same three decades rose from 8.1 per cent to 19.6 per cent. This last, the ratio of G to GNP in 1957, was substantially greater than the corresponding ratio in 1939 (14.6 per cent) and greater also than the 1947-1951 ratios

---

of the value of such governmentally produced intermediate services, all G will be treated as though it were "final." On this count, G overstates the sacrifice in forgone personal consumption and private investment.

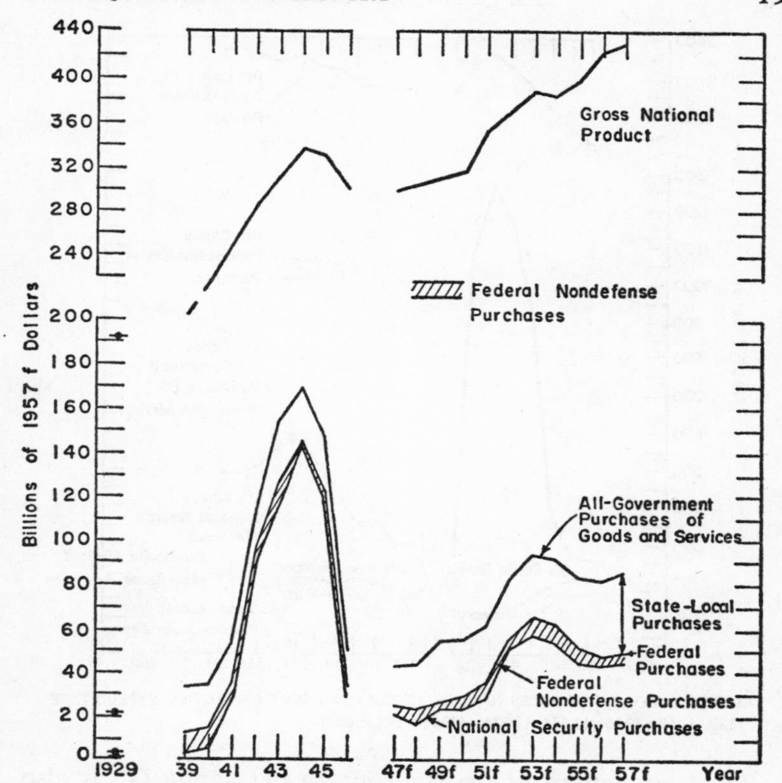

CHART 1 GROSS NATIONAL PRODUCT AND GOVERNMENT PURCHASES OF GOODS AND SERVICES, 1929, 1939-1946, 1947f-1957f (BILLIONS OF 1957f DOLLARS)

(12.7-15.9 per cent). On the other hand, it is well below the 23 per cent share of government in GNP during the height of the Korean War effort in 1953, and cannot compare with the 1943 ratio, when government exhaustive spending took 46 per cent of the national output (see Column 12 of Table 3).[2]

[2] The above ratios are of G to GNP rather than of G* to GNP*. For technical reasons the ratio of two undeflated figures which belong to the same year is a better indicator of what is wanted than are the "deflated" ratios. (It happens that the G*/GNP* ratio increased less be-

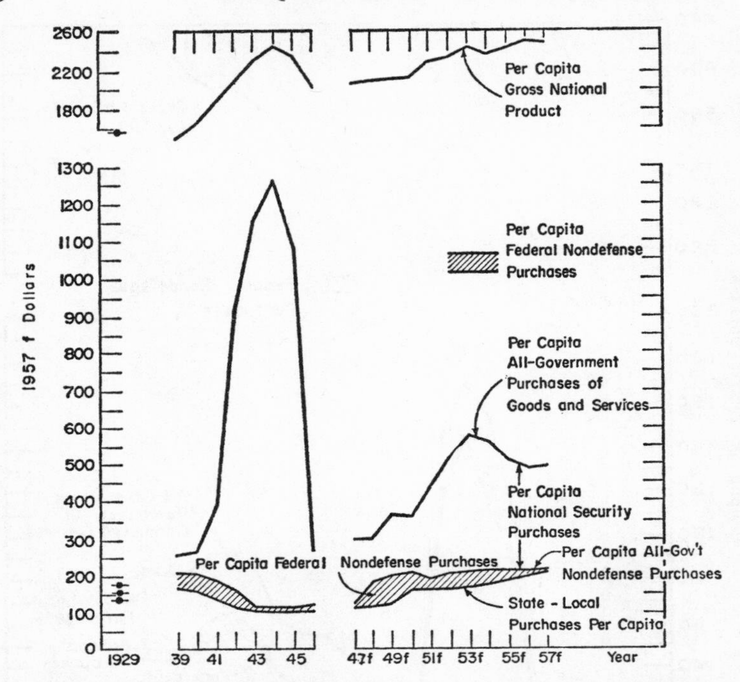

CHART 2. PER CAPITA GROSS NATIONAL PRODUCT AND GOV'T EXHAUSTIVE EXPENDITURE 1929, 1939 - 1946, 1947f - 1957f (1957f DOLLARS)

The time pattern of the statistics on per capita G* is also what one might expect, given the weight of defense during the war and since 1949 (Chart 2). During the 1930's, G* per head rose, albeit in zigzag fashion, from $169 in 1929 to $256 in 1939. Then came the wartime years of rapid expansion; by 1944 annual government purchases of goods and services in real terms hit a peak of $1,223 for every head of population. With demobilization, G* per capita fell to $300 in 1947 (17

tween 1929 and 1957 than the G/GNP ratio—from 10.6 per cent [rather than 8.1 per cent] to 19.6 per cent. The prices of G-type goods rose more than the average of all final-product prices.)

per cent higher than in 1939), only to rise again to a postwar high of $587 during the Korean War (1953). And, although the Eisenhower administration managed by means of federal economies following the armistice to make G* per capita fall —to $498 in 1957, the 1957 level still exceeded that in 1947 by two-thirds. "Real" all-government exhaustive expenditure per head rose faster in the defense-ridden postwar decade than during the depression.

Nondefense Totals

The series on total government purchases is not a bad guide to the history of spending for defense and war, but it leaves hidden the rather more intriguing story of public expenditure for other than security.[3] Instead of the fourfold increase shown by total G* between 1929 and 1957, *nondefense* public spending in real terms only a little more than doubled, rising from $18.9 billion in 1929 to $39.8 billion in 1957. Moreover, when matched against the rise in nondefense gross national product, i.e., against the rise in the total nondefense output of the economy, the *share* of government increased only from 7.5 per cent in 1929 to 10.3 per cent in 1957. Indeed, the ratio of nondefense G to nondefense GNP during the postwar years remained well below the 1939 and 1940 figures of 13.4 per cent and 12 per cent. It appears, in other words, that of the resources left over for private and public "civilian" consump-

[3] Charts 1 and 2 and Columns 1-8 of Table 4 contain the relevant figures: "total national security" expenditure (TNS) in current and in deflated (1957) prices (TNS*); nondefense public expenditure, i.e., G* minus TNS*; nondefense G* per capita; nondefense GNP*, total, per capita, and per household; and the share of nondefense G in nondefense GNP. TNS is equivalent to what the Department of Commerce labels "national security" (adjusted to a net-of-sales basis [see note b, Table 4]). It includes in addition to the Budget Bureau's "national defense" and "international affairs and finance plus defense support" some expenditures on the merchant marine. GNP* minus TNS* measures the volume of total output available for nondefense use.

tion and capital formation—left over, that is, after military provision for survival—we have been committing in the postwar period only a slightly larger fraction to such communal uses as schools, roads, sanitation, urban renewal, etc., than we did in 1929, and a smaller share than in 1939 and 1940. (In calendar 1953, the one postwar year for which I have comparable estimates, the share of government in nondefense output—the ratio of nondefense G to nondefense GNP—was lower in the United States than, e.g., in capitalist West Germany (15.1 per cent), welfare conscious England (14.5 per cent), socialist Sweden (14.3 per cent), and capitalist Belgium (11.7 per cent). As among the six countries for which I made the calculation, only the Canadian ratio (10.6 per cent) was lower than our 11.2 per cent (with only national-defense-proper subtracted). Our 1957 ratio of 10.8 per cent was just barely higher than Canada's. [For other comparative figures see the section on international comparisons and Table 14.])[4]

The *per capita* figures of real nondefense spending are also of interest. (See Chart 2 and Column 4, Table 4.) During the 1930's, nondefense G* per head of population rose from $155 in 1929 to $233 in 1939. After a wartime decline to $118 (in 1945) it began to rise once again, passing its 1929 level in 1947 but remaining well below the 1939 figure of $233 until 1954, when it hit $236. But 1954 marks the record. In 1955 and also in 1957 nondefense G* per head fell off again, if only a little. In 1957, at $234 we devoted about the same volume of resources per head of population to civilian-type public use as in 1939 despite the fact that total (real) civilian output per capita had risen from $1,514 in 1939 to $2,281 in 1957.

[4] During World War II public G-type spending for other than defense fell both in absolute amount (in real terms) and as a proportion of nondefense GNP; we cut back *communal* civilian consumption and investment more than personal consumption. During the Korean War, however, nondefense G* and the proportion of nondefense G to nondefense GNP fell only between 1950 and 1951 and then only slightly.

(Nondefense GNP* per *household* was $7,826 in 1957; of this we devoted $803 to *public* consumption and investment. The corresponding 1940 figures were $6,117 and $840.)[5]

Federal vs. State-Local Civilian Purchases[6]

What in all this has been the role of the federal government? Spending for national security is, of course, virtually all federal. But what about exhaustive spending on other than defense—e.g., on conservation, public health, and public works? Do the figures indicate a trend of federal budgetary encroachment on state-local civilian functions?

Whatever the trend, the federal share in nondefense exhaustive spending is strikingly small; of all civilian-type G, the federal government was the source of only 8.1 per cent in 1929 and 12.2 per cent in 1957. True, in most peacetime years in between, the proportion was considerably higher: 33 per cent

[5] The 1939-1957 per capita comparison is not affected even if one adds to real nondefense purchases of goods and services the somewhat ambiguous category of spending which the Commerce Department labels "subsidies less surplus of government enterprises" (adjusted for price level change). In 1939 the *sum* of real public purchases and subsidies came to $242 per capita; the corresponding 1957 figure was $241. On the other hand, in 1954 all-government "subsidies less surplus" was negative; the sum of the two categories amounted to only $232, *less* than in 1957. However, to compare the $241 in 1957 with $232 in 1954 is to overstate the difference. Much of the increase in "subsidies less surplus" between 1954 and 1957 was due to the agricultural price-support operations of the Commodity Credit Corporation, some of which involved the finance of foreign aid through the disposal, at a loss, of surplus crops via the so-called Public Law 480 program. If one adds to purchases only nondefense subsidies, the 1957 total comes to about $239. (On the handling of "subsidies less surplus," see notes on pp. 10, 14; on the treatment of C.C.C. operations, the note on p. 36. To deflate "subsidies less surplus" I used the Commerce Department's implicit deflator for "foreign marketings and C.C.C. loans" and the deflator for GNP, in appropriate mixture.)

[6] See Charts 1 and 2 and Columns 4-7 of Table 5 for the figures on nondefense FG* (total and per capita) and for the ratios of nondefense FG to nondefense G and nondefense GNP.

or so in 1939 and 1940; 20-28 per cent in the late 1940's; 23 per cent in 1953 and 1954. But since 1954 Washington's percentage has been falling fast; in 1957 it was only a little over a third of what it had been in 1939-1940 and lower than in any year for which the figures are available (1929, 1939-1957) save 1929 and 1945. Even if one takes into account that some state and local exhaustive expenditure is financed by federal grants-in-aid—and that in 1957 the state-local share in nondefense G was less (by a twentieth!) than in 1929—these figures hardly suggest an imminent federal "take-over." (As a matter of fact, even if one takes *total* G, defense and all, Washington's fractional share has fallen in every year since 1953; in 1957, at 58.7 per cent, it was no higher than in 1947-1950.)[7]

What about the *absolute* level of federal civilian purchases? In 1929 Washington absorbed $13 of a per capita nondefense

[7] The federal share in the combined total of public nondefense purchases *plus* "subsidies less surplus of government enterprises" has been rather greater: 9.1 per cent in 1929; 38-40 per cent in 1939-1940; 26-31 per cent in the late 1940's; 26 per cent, 20 per cent, 21 per cent, and 19 per cent in 1954-1957. Even in the combined total, however, and despite the big rise in federal agricultural subsidies in 1957, the federal government's share in 1957 was half of what it had been in 1939-1940, and fell by a fourth between 1954 and 1957. It was also lower than in any of the years 1929, 1939-1957, except, of course, 1929. (Note that these are not truly nondefense statistics: except for 1954-1957 I have no way of knowing how much of "subsidies less surplus" was defense-connected; hence all the above figures are based on the totals given in Table 2, appropriately adjusted for price change.)

Federal vs. state-local comparisons are, of course, complicated by federal grants-in-aid to state and local governments. The Department of Commerce treats all such grants as federal *nonexhaustive* expenditure; grant financed state-local exhaustive spending is booked as SG. Yet to the extent that federal grants-in-aid are ear-marked for specific kinds of exhaustive spending (e.g., highways), the question of which level of government really absorbs the resources is meaningless: decision and control are shared. Since the actual administering and purchasing are apt to be by state-local governments, and also because I do not have data on what proportion of federal grants-in-aid is tied to specific kinds of purchases by the recipient, I here follow Commerce Department practice.

GNP* of $1,573. By 1957, civilian output had grown to $2,281 per head; the federal government's share, at $29, had increased somewhat faster. But $29 was hardly a record. In 1939 and 1940 the total of real nondefense federal purchases had been $71 per capita, and in all nonwar years since then, save two, it ranged between $35 and $56. Moreover, the 1954-1957 trend was sharply negative. (The percentage share of the federal government in civilian GNP in 1957, at 1.3 per cent, was a third of what it had been in 1939 and 1940 and at its lowest level, save 1951, since 1946. Per *household,* federal nondefense spending in 1957 took $98 of a total civilian output of $7,826; in 1940 the corresponding figures were $270 and $6,117.)[8]

[8] The size of the decline in real federal civilian purchases between 1954 and 1957—from $55 to $29 per capita (Table 5)—is misleading. About four-fifths or so of the decline reflects a sharp fall in G-type expenditure on agriculture, a fall which was in part offset by a rise in federal agricultural subsidies. However, even if one adds federal "subsidies less surplus" (appropriately deflated) to federal nondefense purchases of goods and services, the resulting series shows a sharp downward trend between 1954 and 1957 (from $60 per capita to $46) and a very sharp decline from the 1939 total of $87. (With agricultural foreign-aid subsidy taken out, the 1957 figure is $44; there was no such subsidy in 1954. The section on "functional shares" below contains an explanation of how agricultural price-support operations are treated in the national income accounts.)

It should be noted that the broad pattern of the history of nondefense FG* is not at all sensitive to small variations in the statistics, i.e., to variations of, say, $1—$4 on a per capita basis. This is important, because the FG* minus TNS* (total national security) series is of slightly dubious ancestry. TNS was deflated not by an index of its own (I know of none), but by the index for FG. Since most of FG is made up of TNS, the *relative* distortion in TNS* is almost certainly negligible. But a given absolute error that is small in relation to a large number could be substantial relative to a small number; hence results based on fine differences in FG* minus TNS* would have to be taken with a grain of salt. On the other hand, the nondefense ratios of FG to G and to GNP are based on current-price series, hence are not on this account distorted. The all-government series, too, are relatively immune—civilian FG constitutes only a small fraction of nondefense G.

Functional Shares: 1957

To people conditioned to think of public spending as a euphemism for waste the fact that there has been since 1939—in fact, since 1929—no substantial rise in the fractional share of government in civilian output is of small comfort; any increase in the absolute magnitude of G is bad. But the open-minded might be inclined to explore further. On what kinds of things has the government spent our money?

Table 6 contains a detailed breakdown by function of federal and state-local purchases of goods and services in *calendar* 1957. (Chart 3 shows the breakdown as among broad categories.) Of the all-government total of $87.1 billion, some $44.6 billion went for *national defense* proper and $2.1 billion for *international affairs and finance* (i.e., for conduct of foreign affairs, "informational activities," and foreign economic assistance plus defense support [$1.8 billion]). In all, 53 per cent of government purchases of goods and services in 1957 was accounted for by these two "national security" categories, with the federal government responsible for virtually all.[9]

By far the largest "civilian" item was *education*. It absorbed $13.6 billion—33 per cent of nondefense public purchases. All but $.1 billion of this was state and local G, but the federal contribution was augmented by some $.27 billion in grants-in-aid. (Of the $13.6 billion, which came to around $280 per household, $8.8 billion went for wages and salaries, $2.8 billion for construction, and $2 billion for "other purchases."

[9] The sum of the two categories is somewhat less than "total national security" (when TNS is gross of sales). Expenditure on the merchant marine, for instance, is included in TNS, while in Table 6 it is classified under "water transportation" in the "commerce and housing" category. (It should be noted, incidentally, that the percentages given in the text are relative to G gross of sales, i.e., $87.554 billion. The reason is that the functional components are available only on a "gross of sales" basis. The sum of the components will not exactly equal the given totals because of rounding.)

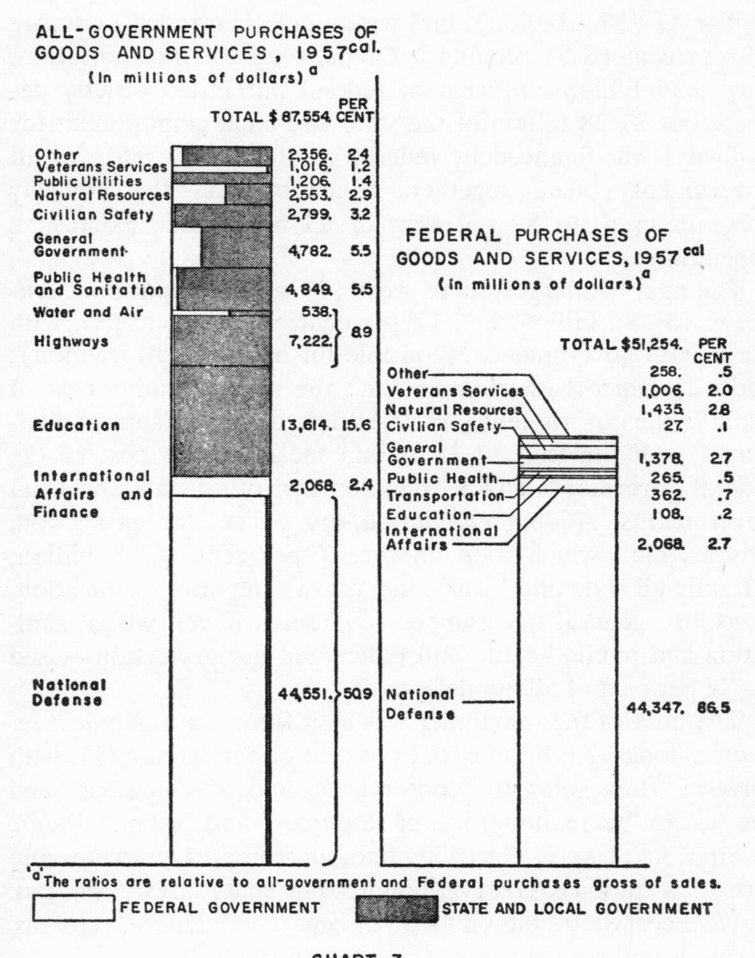

CHART 3

Eleven and four tenths billion dollars represented the cost of primary and secondary education.

The second largest civilian item, *transportation,* cost $7.76 billion, with the highway program taking 18 per cent of all civilian G ($7.2 billion), and water and air transport another 1.3 per cent ($.54 billion).[10] Of the total for transportation, only $.36 billion consisted of federal purchases, strictly defined; but $1.28 billion of the state and local commitment for highways was financed by federal grant. At any rate, for all governments taken together, education and the highway program used up 52 per cent of all nondefense exhaustive expenditure.

The next two largest items were (1) *public health and sanitation* ($4.85 billion, i.e., 12 per cent of nondefense G, with the federal government responsible for only a small fraction); and (2) *general government*, i.e., the administrative cost of running the government ($4.78 billion, or 12 per cent of civilian G). Of the last, $1.38 billion measures the cost of the federal government and $3.4 billion that of all state and local governments. Adding *civilian safety:* police, fire protection, prisons, etc., which took another 7 per cent ($2.8 billion, virtually all state and local), the above categories—education, transport, general government (overhead, if you wish), sanitation and public health, and police and fire protection—used up 82 per cent of all nondefense G.

The bulk of the remainder was split three ways. *Natural resources* took $2.6 billion (6.2 per cent of nondefense G), with three-quarters going to "conservation and development" and the rest to "recreational use of resources" and "other." *Public utilities,* i.e., transit, electricity and, most important, water and gas, took another $1.21 billion (3 per cent). Last, *veterans' services* cost $1.02 billion (2.5 per cent), with federal veterans' hospitals and medical care taking four-fifths.[11]

[10] In addition to expenditure on the merchant marine, the "water transport" category includes spending on harbor construction, inland waterways, etc. Air transport, in turn, covers C.A.A. activities, construction and operation of civilian airfields, etc.

[11] Exhaustive expenditure on agriculture in calendar 1957 was only $.26 billion. The rest of the $3 billion of spending on agriculture con-

Functional Shares: 1947-1957

Table 7 contains figures for *fiscal* 1947-1957 of federal purchases of goods and services classified by major Budget Bureau function, and a comparable breakdown of state-local and all-government purchases for 1948, 1950, and 1952-1957. Tables 8, 9, 10, and 11, in turn, give the ratios of the functional components to total exhaustive expenditure, to nondefense G, to GNP, and to nondefense GNP.[12]

---

sisted of subsidies. For discussion of the treatment of C.C.C. price-support operations, see the section on Agriculture (p. 35).

Since this book was first written (in the summer and autumn of 1958) the Commerce Department has completed and published a series on the functional composition of government purchases which covers, in addition to 1957, the years 1952-1956 (*U.S. Income and Output,* 1958). The major changes in the composition of G between calendar 1952 and 1957 were as follows: the share of defense plus international affairs fell from 63 per cent to 53 per cent; the share of education in nondefense G rose from 27.6 per cent to 33.3 per cent; that of highways from 15.8 per cent to 17.6 per cent; veterans' services fell from 4.2 per cent to 2.5 per cent; and G-type expenditure on agriculture from 3.6 per cent to .6 per cent (after reaching 12 per cent in 1953). Besides national defense, absolute declines occurred in the dollar amounts devoted to international affairs and finance, to veterans' services, to exhaustive expenditure on agriculture, to "water transport," and to "housing and community redevelopment." (Spending on the last fell from $581 million in 1952 to $185 million in 1957.) All such absolute declines are especially significant since they occurred in the face of rising prices and hence indicate much larger "real" reductions.

[12] The fiscal 1947-1957 series in Table 7, which were constructed before the publication of the Department of Commerce data for calendar 1952-1957, are based on a much cruder classification of functions than the Commerce tables but cover a longer period. (Time series of exhaustive expenditure by function are not easy to come by. The Commerce Department series go back only to 1952; and the Budget Bureau, while it publishes very fine functional breakdowns for the federal government, lumps exhaustive expenditure with nonexhaustive spending and with loans. Table 7 is based on some unpublished esti-

The best way to find out about the functional composition of government purchases since 1947 is to study the tables. Nonetheless, the following summary comments may be useful:

1. *Defense* dominates not only the federal but also the all-government total. Spending for "major national security" exclusive of the "defense support" type of foreign aid took anywhere from about 30 per cent of all government purchases (in 1949 and 1950) to 59 per cent (in 1952 and 1953), with the lowest post-Korea ratio, in 1956, at 49.3 per cent (Column 1, Table 8). The ratio of "major national security" to total *federal* purchases ranged between a postwar low of 51 per cent in 1949, a Korean War peak of 85.1 per cent in 1952, and a 1957 ratio of 85.5 per cent. The post-Korea figures (through 1957) were all above 83 per cent.[13]

Ratios fluctuate according to what happens to the denominator as well as to the numerator; to find out about the scale of the defense effort, one must look at the absolute figures in Table 7 and consider also that the prices of defense goods have risen by roughly 45 per cent since 1947. In absolute terms, the price-corrected figures for major national security (less defense support) rose from a postwar low in 1948 of $15.3 billion to a peak of $55.5 billion during the Korean War (in 1953), then

---

mates of the composition of federal G prepared from Budget Bureau data by Mr. Samuel M. Cohn, Mrs. Naomi Sweeney, and Mr. Charles Stockman, all of the Bureau; and on Census Bureau data for state-local governments.)

The reader who has had a surfeit of statistics might read only about those functional categories in which he has a particular interest and then turn to the last two sections of the chapter ("Government Capital Formation" and "Comparison with Other Countries").

[13] "Major national security" less "defense support" is a category of the Budget Bureau. It should not be confused with "*total* national security," which, in addition to "major national security," includes "international affairs and finance including defense support" as well as exhaustive spending on the merchant marine, on civil defense, and on veterans' life insurance trust funds.

fell to $42-44 billion in 1955-1957 (Column 11, Table 7). These figures are not entirely comparable with those available for 1940-1945. However, the series for "*total* national security" does go back. It appears that in terms of absolute scale of effort we are devoting to security less than one-third of what we allocated in 1944—out of a GNP* more than a fourth greater than in 1944. ("Major national security" has taken in the postwar period between 4.5 per cent and 13.7 per cent of GNP, in 1948 and 1953 respectively, with 1956 and 1957 at a little under 10 per cent.)

2. Spending on *international affairs and finance* has ranged from a high of $5.3 billion in 1949 to post-Korea figures of $1.6–$2.1 billion (Column 2, Table 7. Since the figures are not corrected for change in the price level, those for earlier years substantially understate the volume of aid in terms of 1957 prices).[14] A relatively small though rising amount (from $.12 billion in 1947 to $.29 billion in 1957) went for "conduct of foreign affairs" and for "informational activities." The bulk of the money, however, was used for two categories of foreign aid: defense support and economic aid proper. Together these two kinds of aid came to $2+ billion in 1947 and 1948, reached $5.1 billion in the peak Marshall Plan year of 1949, and then fell to post-Korea levels of $1.4–$1.9 billion (1954-1957). In relation to total output, defense support plus economic aid fell from pre-Korea ratios of 0.9–2.0 per cent to 0.4–0.5 per cent in 1953-1957. Moreover, during 1952-1957 (the only years for which the breakdown is available) defense support made up 68–93 per cent of the total, leaving for economic aid proper amounts ranging from $.2 billion in 1952 to $.5 billion

[14] I did not attempt to put together price-corrected figures for the civilian components of G. There exist no appropriate price indices, and, given how little usable information there is about the commodity composition of expenditures by function, I did not venture to construct any.

in 1957 (Column 3, Table 7). Nondefense economic aid used up between .05–.12 per cent of GNP.[15]

3. *Labor and welfare,* the largest nondefense component of G, consists of spending for education, for sanitation, public health, and hospitals, for "promotion of science, research, libraries and museums," for parks and recreation, for penal institutions, and for the administration of public assistance programs (Column 5, Table 7). Exhaustive expenditure on all these functions taken together rose steadily from $8.7 billion in 1948 to $21.4 billion in 1957, with the total taking (1) an increasing share of GNP (3.5 per cent in 1948 and 4.9 per cent in 1957); (2) a faster increasing share of nondefense GNP (3.7 per cent in 1948 and 5.5 per cent in 1957); and (3) a rising share of nondefense G (43.3 per cent to 51.3 per cent). Very little of purchases in the "labor and welfare" category is federal; between 1947 and 1957 Washington's share grew from $0.3 billion to only $0.5 billion, and less than $1 billion of state-local *exhaustive* spending in 1957 was financed by federal grants-in-aid. *State-local* spending on labor and welfare, on the other hand, has made up 55–58 per cent of all state-local purchases during most of the postwar period (no trend), with the bill for education alone running to $5.4 billion in 1948 and $14.5 billion in 1957 (i.e., well over a third of all SG).[16]

[15] Spending on international affairs and finance ranged from 7.1 per cent to 12.9 per cent of G before Korea, and from 1.9 per cent to 2.7 per cent after 1953; the corresponding ratios to FG were 11.8–21.4 per cent and 2.9–4.4 per cent. The share of economic aid proper in G has varied from 0.2 per cent to 0.6 per cent; in FG it grew from 0.3 per cent in 1952 to 1 per cent in 1957.

[16] Table 12 contains Census Bureau data on public expenditure (G) on education, split between "higher" and primary-secondary; and on the ratio of the total to G, to nondefense G, to GNP, and to nondefense GNP. In interpreting the figures, especially the ratios to GNP, it is important to bear in mind that productivity (per teacher and per cubic foot of classroom space) rises much more slowly in the "production" of education than in the production of most other things (e.g., cars, radios, etc.). It follows that in order to maintain the "output" of "education"

4. Spending on the second largest civilian category, *commerce and housing,* also increased, from $3.8 billion in 1948 to $9.5 billion in 1957 (Column 8, Table 7). These amounts cover all public spending on transportation, on public housing and community development, on civil defense, and on "regulation of commerce and finance," with spending for highways taking between 75-85 per cent of the total. The percentage share of commerce and housing in all-government nondefense purchases rose from 19 per cent in 1948 to 23 per cent in 1957; its share in civilian GNP, in turn, increased from 1.6 per cent in 1948 to 2.5 per cent in 1957. Only $.6–$.9 billion of the total has been federal G, but the federal *financial* contribution in the form of grants-in-aid has been substantial. (The share of federal exhaustive spending on commerce and housing in total civilian FG has fluctuated widely [3–18 per cent]; the corresponding state-local ratio, i.e., the percentage share of commerce and housing in total SG, grew from 21 per cent in 1948 to 24 per cent in 1957.)

5. *General government,* so called, is the third largest nondefense category of exhaustive expenditure. Covering such things as "legislative and judicial functions," "federal financial management," etc., it reflects the government's overhead. In absolute terms, the cost of government also increased, from $4.4 billion in 1948 to $7.4 billion in 1957. But there has been quite a lot of "spreading" of the overhead; the share in G of general government fell from 13 per cent in 1948 to 8.6 per cent in 1957, with, however, a rise in recent years from a low

---

in constant proportion to the output of other things, spending for education relative to spending for all other things must rise; i.e., some rise in the fraction of "education" to GNP has been necessary just to stay even, quite apart from the rise in enrollment in relation to population. Moreover, any discussion about the share of education should take account of the possibility that at higher income levels people would *want* to devote a larger fraction of their income to education.

of 6.6 per cent in 1953. The federal component has ranged from \$1.1 billion to \$1.7 billion, with 1947 at \$1.3 billion and 1957 at \$1.7 billion. The fractional share of the federal government in the total of general government dropped (from 29.5 per cent in 1948 to 23 per cent in 1957); in relation to total federal purchases, federal overhead fell dramatically from 7.3 per cent in 1947 to 2.2 per cent in 1954, with a subsequent rise to 3.4 per cent in 1957. (This is the pattern one would expect, of course, with the sharp rise and then the slow decline in defense spending.) In relation to GNP, general government fell from 1.8 per cent in 1948 to 1.5 per cent in 1953, then rose to 1.7 per cent in 1957. In relation to civilian GNP, it remained at 1.8–1.9 per cent.

6. Between 1948 and 1957 commerce and housing, labor and welfare, and general government together accounted for between 84-92 per cent of civilian G, with the proportion rising during the decade. The remainder went for natural resources, agriculture, and *veterans' services*. The last, most of it medical, fell from 7.5 per cent of nondefense G in 1947 to 2.6 per cent in 1957, with even the absolute amount declining (despite inflation) from a postwar peak of \$1.9+ billion in 1947 to \$1.1 billion in 1957. All but about \$0.1 billion per year was federal; it constituted 49 per cent of all nondefense FG in 1947, 14 per cent in 1954, and (with the dollar amount remaining constant) 21 per cent in 1957. The total burden fell from 0.6 per cent of civilian GNP in 1948 to 0.3 per cent in 1957.

7. *Natural resources* expenditure, mostly on "conservation and development of forest-, mineral-, land-, water-, and animal-resources," rose from something less than \$1 billion in 1948 to \$1.9 billion in 1957, constituting a 4-6 per cent share of civilian G (with no trend). Between two-thirds and three-quarters of this was federal, accounting for a widely fluctuating 13-25 per cent of nondefense FG (with 1951, however, at 34

per cent, due to a large drop in federal civilian spending).

8. The last category is *agriculture,* and includes such expenditures for net additions to Commodity Credit Corporation (C.C.C.) inventories and to outstanding commodity "loans," on Federal Housing Administration activities in agriculture, on conservation, and on research and extension services as are classified as purchases of goods and services by the Department of Commerce. The resulting series shows no trend but is the most volatile of the lot, ranging from −$1.1 billion to +$3.3 billion. The fluctuations are largely due to the uneven incidence, year by year, of commodity purchases and sales by the C.C.C., and of the balance between repayment by farmers and new loans by the C.C.C. against commodity collateral (which the Department of Commerce sensibly books as *de facto* purchase by the C.C.C.). At its peak, in 1954, the $3 billion total of federal G on agriculture constituted a substantial 39 per cent of civilian FG, but in 1955 and 1956 the amount fell to $1.3 billion and in 1957 it vanished. (It does not follow, of course, that total federal spending on agriculture fell to zero. It happened, however, that in 1957 all such outlay was made up of outright subsidies, e.g., soil-bank payments, or of noncommodity loans by, for instance, the Rural Electrification Administration.)[17]

[17] I do not have a figure for *total* federal spending on agriculture in fiscal 1957. (The figure given in the *U.S. Budget* is a hybrid and not comparable to the Commerce Department's "income and product"-type statistics used throughout this book. Among other things, the timing of the entries is quite different [see note b, Table 1].) However, the Commerce Department does provide calendar year figures. During calendar 1957 federal agricultural "subsidies less surplus" came to $2.7 billion; net agricultural purchases were negative. In calendar 1956 the corresponding figures were $2.2 billion and −$.1 billion. In contrast, agricultural subsidies in calendar 1953 accounted for only $.5 billion of a total expenditure on agriculture of $4.2 billion. (The Department of Commerce books as purchases of goods and services not only additions to C.C.C.-owned inventories and increases in outstanding C.C.C.

Government Capital Formation

Unfortunately, the United States national income accounts do not distinguish between public consumption and public investment. Yet a surprisingly large share of government exhaustive expenditure is for durable equipment and construction —hardly a trivial fact when it comes to comparison, say, of American and Russian investment rates.[18]

Table 13 contains rough estimates of public investment for 1952-1957 as derived from Census data. It appears that during 1952-1957 somewhere between 31 per cent and 36 per cent of G consisted of investment, with a little less than half involving construction. In dollar terms, public investment amounted to a rising total of \$24.4–\$27.6 billion; 30+ per cent of both FG and SG was on capital account. Defense, of course, accounts for a lot of public investment (between 54 per cent and 66 per cent of the total). But the all-government *ratio* of investment to total purchases is not altered much by eliminating defense; nondefense public investment used up about 28-34 per cent of civilian G. The ratio of federal civilian investment

loans against commodity collateral but also increases in privately financed but C.C.C.-guaranteed loans. It handles these as though they involved outright C.C.C. purchase of the collateral. Repayment, or sales from C.C.C. stocks, enter G negatively, at book value. Any difference between book value and the price realized on a sale, in turn, is treated as a deficit of a government enterprise, and hence is added to "subsidies less surplus." For the figures, see *U.S. Income and Output,* Department of Commerce, 1958.)

[18] In the United States national income accounts, GNP is split into four major product-components: personal consumption, *net* exports of goods and services, government purchases, and gross private domestic investment. To get a ratio of domestic investment to gross national product comparable to the Russian ratio, one cannot divide by GNP the fourth component alone. The numerator must contain, in addition to what is explicitly labeled investment, at least the investment component of government purchases and perhaps some portion of *durable* "consumption."

to civilian FG, while erratic, appears in most years to have been between 20 and 30 per cent.[19]

Comparison with Other Countries

Table 14 contains some revealing comparative information on public spending in relation to GNP in the United States, West Germany, the United Kingdom, Belgium, Canada, and Sweden. All but the United States figures are for 1952 or 1953—years for which there exist easily comparable totals. For the United States, the table gives 1957 as well as 1953 data since the latter year was quite untypical: due to the Korean War, federal G was $10+ billion higher than in 1955-1957, and about double the pre-Korea levels; and GNP was down, reflecting the recession.

It appears that while the ratio of government purchases to GNP, at 19.6 per cent, was higher in the United States (in 1957) than in all the other five countries (in 1952 and 1953) except the United Kingdom (22.9 per cent), the German ratio

[19] The Commerce Department treatment of capital introduces still another bias into the measurement of exhaustive expenditure. Specifically, it gives rise to an understatement (other things equal) of both G and GNP. While the purchase of an old physical asset, e.g., an old building (as distinct from currently produced or inventoried items), does not constitute a claim on the capacity of the economy to produce goods and services, the implicit rental value of the services of such an asset, once acquired, as of all government-owned assets, does measure such a claim. For want of a good basis for estimating the value of the services rendered by such publicly owned physical assets, the national income accounts ignore public assets which are not employed in producing something for commercial sale. (Unlike in private business, where interest and normal profit are a measure of the capital and entrepreneurial services "used up" in current production, it would be grossly misleading to use government, especially federal, interest, most of which is a heritage of the war. [The figures on personal consumption are biased for analogous reasons. No account is taken of the services of, e.g., household appliances; their full cost is written off in the year of purchase.])

of 19.3 per cent was just barely smaller than ours, and all except the Belgian were over 18 per cent. Moreover, if one takes out defense and looks at the ratio of nondefense G to nondefense GNP, it turns out—as was pointed out above—that the share of government in *civilian* GNP was lower in the United States than in four of the other five countries, with only the Canadian ratio slightly lower than ours. (In 1953, too, we were next to last, with only the Canadian ratio below the United States level.)

The column on government transfer-, interest-, and subsidy-payments, too, is of interest. In relation to GNP, *nonexhaustive* public expenditure in the United States was at a much lower level than in any of the other five countries. The 1957 United States ratio of nonexhaustive spending to GNP of 5.9 per cent compares with 14.4 per cent in Belgium, 12.8 per cent in the United Kingdom, 11.5 per cent in West Germany, 8.4 per cent in Canada, and 7.5 per cent in Sweden. (Our 1953 ratio was 4.8 per cent.) In fact, if one calculates, as is often done, the not very meaningful ratio of *total* public expenditure (E) to GNP as an indicator of the volume of government spending, for whatever purpose, in relation to the size of the economy, the United States 1957 ratio of 25.5 per cent turns out to be the lowest of the lot. The United Kingdom heads the list with 35.7 per cent, but Belgium and West Germany at 31.2 per cent and 30.8 per cent are not far behind; Canada is next with 26.6 per cent, while socialist Sweden, at 25.9 per cent, has a public budget almost as low in relation to GNP as ours. The 1953 United States ratio of 27.4 per cent was somewhat higher than that of the Canadians and the Swedes but lower than the rest (despite the budgetary effect of the Korean War).[20]

[20] Note, incidentally, that despite a much smaller GNP and GNP per capita, the United Kingdom defense effort in 1953, at 9.9 per cent of GNP, was of the same relative size as ours in 1957, substantially higher than even Canada's 8.5 per cent, and much higher than that of her competitor, West Germany (4.9 per cent).

Facts speak, if at all, only for themselves. They can help rid us of spurious conjectures masquerading as well-tested truths, but for light on the big questions: Are we spending too much? Too little? Can we 'afford' to spend more? we must look further, to the sketchily mapped realm of cause, consequence, and value. Part Two is an attempt at partial reconnaissance of this treacherous domain, intended to test the usefulness, in lieu of a map, of three popular rules of thumb: "stop inflation," "cater to the consumer," and "avoid coercion."

Part Two

ISSUES

4 INFLATION

SINCE 1945 we have seen a lot of inflation (the consumer price index in 1957 was at 144 per cent of its 1946 value) and a lot of government spending. It is not surprising that in the "public mind" there has formed an impression of a necessary connection—especially since there has been a connection. Government spending has certainly contributed to that excess of total spending over the capacity of the economy to produce goods and services which has been the proximate cause of inflation (at least until 1957). What bears examination is the belief—widely held on the level of popular journalism and the political speech—that the postwar inflation was an unavoidable consequence of the level of public spending.

The proposition that public spending leads to inflation has many variants. The crudest, that any increase in government spending, from whatever level, is bound to cause inflation, has the merit of asserting something that can be tested against the facts. So tested, it turns out to be wrong (as in 1929-1931, 1937-1939, 1948-1949).[1]

[1] In all those years both the wholesale and the consumer price index, as also the implicit deflator for GNP, were falling, while all-government and federal total expenditures (E) and purchases (G) were rising, bar only federal G between 1938 and 1939. Recall that G stands for

A less foolish variant holds that the price level will rise if G (or *total* public spending, E) grows faster than GNP. The implication is that any increase in the public share of total output (or in the ratio of total government spending to GNP) necessarily causes inflation. Again, the facts refute the hypothesis (e.g., in 1930-1933, 1937-1938, and 1948-1949).

There is a third, more slippery version, according to which there is an absolute ceiling on the ratio of government spending to GNP above which inflation is unavoidable. Trivially true (at least for G) at 100 per cent, the proposition is of course empty unless the critical ratio is specified. Recently, the most popular specification has been that of Colin Clark; 25 per cent as the threshold to doom has had quite a remarkable run thanks to Clark's sponsorship. But the facts are again unkind; 25 per cent (or 26 per cent, or 27 per cent) does not hold up.[2]

What if the figures were consistent with one or another conjecture of the above sort? Would it then be sensible to conclude that there is an unbreakable link between public spending and price inflation? Surely not. Inflation, to the extent that it is sensitive to spending, has to do with the balance between the supply of and the demand for scarce resources, between the capacity to produce goods and services and the level of *total* spending for such goods and services. Any proposition which links the price level to public spending alone, or to public spending in relation to *actual* GNP, is faulty at the core; it leaves out of account the two other elements which together with G de-

---

public *exhaustive* expenditure and E for *total* government spending (cf. p. 9. For the prewar data on expenditure see Table 1; for 1948-1949, see sources cited in Table 1. The price indices are from the *Economic Report of the President,* 1958. In making the test I used calendar years for the postwar as well as the prewar period to save having to compute price series by fiscal year.)

[2] At least not as regards total spending. Actually, Clark argues his case in terms of taxes as a proportion of national income. For a brief look at the logic and the evidence, see pp. 50 ff.

termine the balance: the capacity-level of GNP, and the rate of *private* spending.[3]

There may, of course, exist lines of activity where capacity to produce for government account in the short run is a fixed quantity independent of private spending. Moreover, if this were the case for all G, it would be sufficient to look at G alone; putting it crudely, if G exceeded G-capacity, G prices would

[3] That is, of private purchases of goods and services. Except where otherwise indicated, "spending" refers in all that follows to exhaustive expenditure, i.e., to demand for goods and services. "Capacity," in turn, is used to denote not a full-mobilization ceiling but an efficient, business-as-usual intensity of operation: no physical bottlenecks of a major sort, unit costs close to their minima, etc. A complicated notion, capacity is a function of such things as the existing stock of physical capital (plant, machinery, inventories), the state of the management and production arts, the supply and quality of labor, and the output-mix. (Anyone concerned about the good sense of denoting what are really many numbers by a single number and of using prices to make the many numbers commensurate should consult a good textbook on economic theory, e.g., Paul Samuelson's *Economics* [McGraw-Hill, 1958].)

The wary reader may also be concerned with the qualification in the text: "to the extent that (inflation) is sensitive to spending . . ." It is designed to fend off, for the moment, the analytically intricate problem of "cost-push" inflation, i.e., the possibility that wage-price bargains in imperfectly competitive markets will cause the price level to rise even though total money spending is less than the "full-employment" capacity of the economy to produce goods and services. As 1957 has shown, this can happen even if one is conservative in defining full-employment so as to leave plenty of slack both in labor markets and in the rate of plant utilization. The Appendix contains comments on the links between this kind of inflation-during-recession and government spending and taxing; here I confine discussion to inflation due to an inflationary gap between spending and capacity. I do so not only because it simplifies the exposition but also because I believe, and argue in the Appendix, that if one is concerned not with rapid shifting of resources from private to public use under forced draft but with the "steady state" blend of public and private spending, then the relation of capacity to total exhaustive spending is the significant link between the budget and the price level. At any rate, to avoid ambiguity it may be helpful in what follows to think of capacity-operation as leaving whatever slack may be necessary to sap wage-price exuberance.

rise. But there is no such thing as G-capacity. Ford's capacity to produce command cars and jeeps depends in part on the demands made on its facilities by private buyers of trucks and convertibles. The same is true of capacity to produce almost anything else: steel, machine tools, chemicals, food, typewriters, clerical services. Aside from a handful of items in more or less fixed supply which are specific to a military use and have no good substitutes, the scarcity of most resources is affected by private as well as public demand, and the pressure on price depends on the balance between capacity and the total of demand.

It follows that an increase in government spending will cause inflation only if (1) there does not initially exist sufficient unused capacity to accommodate the extra demand (where "capacity" is defined to leave whatever slack may be necessary to avoid bottlenecks and cost-push problems) and (2) if the margin of additional spending over unused capacity is not offset by a compression of private spending sufficient to release the necessary resources. If there is enough slack initially, or if private spending can be compressed, no inflation need occur.[4]

[4] Keeping in mind, however, that: (a) The situation in question is not a high-tempo shift of resources from private to public use. Large shifts require considerable substitution and conversion, and if hurried are bound to create bottleneck difficulties which can easily react on the price level. Indeed, in a world where prices are flexible only upward, some rise in price indices is implied by the very working of the price mechanism; this, in turn, may trigger undesirable second-round effects (cf. p. 122 ff. in Appendix). (b) In calculating the balance between public plus private demand and capacity, one must take into account the effect of extra public spending on the level of *private* spending for goods and services. With unchanged tax rates, an increase in either public purchases (G) or in public nonexhaustive expenditure (N) will cause private incomes to rise and hence will induce additional *private* spending. The extra claim on resources will consist of the increment in G *plus* the G-induced or N-induced increment in private spending. (As regards the spending-capacity balance, the difference between G and N is that $1 of extra G not only induces additional private spending but in itself constitutes $1 of extra demand, i.e., a $1 claim on resources;

One should not, I think, set much store by the first possibility, that there may exist appreciable *unused* capacity. Though recessions will occur, with intelligent policy there should not often exist very much excess slack, certainly not for long. (If unused capacity warrants mention nonetheless, it is for a different reason. There is a sense in which anyone concerned about the balance between public and private spending should always think in terms of additional capacity, even at a time of full employment. The capacity of the economy is growing and growing fast. With the labor force growing not only in skill but also in size, by approximately 800,000 people each year—a rate of about 1.2 per cent; with private and public capital plant expanding even faster [during 1946-1957 capital stock in manufacturing grew at an average rate of 3.75 per cent per annum]; and with some $10 billion or so going into productivity-boosting research every year, we can comfortably count, on the average and barring only a prolonged recession due to a shortfall in total spending, on a 3-4 per cent increase in capacity every year. From early 1959 levels, this comes to a *yearly* increment of some $14 to $19 billion. How this is to be allocated between various private and public uses—between schools and machine tools, defense and private consumables—is a matter for political choice [see Chapters 5-7]. But it is worth remembering that even if it is desired to have personal consumption and private investment each growing at, say, 4 per cent per

---

additional N also induces private spending but does not itself constitute extra demand. Other things equal, therefore, the effect of G on total exhaustive spending [i.e., on total demand for goods and services] exceeds that of N. [It must not be thought, however, that it is this quantitative difference that justifies the insistence of Part One on the distinction. The really important difference between exhaustive and non-exhaustive spending has to do with their qualitatively different consequences for the allocation of resources between private and public uses. But that is a matter for Chapters 5-7.])

year, there would still exist an annual margin for G of about $2.5–$3.7 billion.)

But what of the second possibility—of *diverting* resources from private to government use without resort to inflation by compressing private demand? Is it possible? Could we have diverted the resources absorbed by government during the postwar period by means other than inflation?

This is the nub of the issue. According to standard economic theory it is possible by increasing taxes and restricting credit to compress private spending (relative to capacity) and hence to accommodate extra government purchases by releasing resources from private use. The minor premise of the proposition that government spending causes inflation is, simply, that such compression of private claims, of personal consumption and private investment, is illegitimate or impossible. If so, the proposition does indeed follow. But is it so? Have we really exhausted, nay, overexhausted, the capacity of the fisc to squeeze private spending?

The Capacity to Tax

Theory holds that consumption expenditure and residential construction are sensitive to income after taxes, to householders' liquidity and holdings of assets, and to the cost and availability of installment and mortgage credit. Business investment—purchase of durable equipment, plant construction, and investment in inventories—is affected by expected profitability and by the availability and cost of funds. According to the usual prescription, then, to depress consumption one should raise excise, sales, and income tax rates and make installment money scarce. To restrain investment, in turn, one can make money generally tight, raise tax rates on corporate profits and capital gains, cut down on programs of mortgage support and accelerated amortization, and the like.

To hold that an increase in government spending in a full-employment situation is bound to cause inflation is to assume that the above techniques for compressing private spending are ineffective or intolerable—or unlikely to be used. For the last, at least, there is good evidence. Since 1945 we have passed through three periods of inflation, two of which were certainly caused by excess demand. It is evident that neither in 1946-1948 nor in 1950-1951 were either the fiscal or the various available monetary devices applied with sufficient vigor to do the job. Politicians are loath to raise tax rates, and it takes hardy central bankers to withstand the clamor and squeeze money really tight.

But this is quite beside the point. For a judgment about the anti-inflationary efficacy and desirability of higher taxes the prediction that politicians will not raise them is irrelevant. It is legitimate enough for the Secretary of the Treasury to base his budgetary calculations on a tactical estimate of what he can get from the Congress, but our concern must be with the other two questions: Is it *possible* by tough-minded application of the fiscal and monetary powers of government to compress private spending and thereby to release resources for public use without causing price inflation? If so, would the consequent damage in terms of important values be so great as to warrant the conclusion that "it shouldn't be done"?[5]

[5] Note that the second question concerns the desirability of using taxes and tight money for the purpose of releasing resources from private use *when no idle resources are to be had*. There is still a third question, notably whether it is always wise to apply enough monetary and fiscal pressure on demand to keep prices from rising even when ample resources are idle. If a rise in the consumer price index always signaled an excess of spending over capacity, the question would not arise. But in a world of cost-push, where, moreover, price indices are loaded with semi-publicly administered prices such as rents and transport rates, such indices are poor indicators of the balance between spending and capacity, and a policy sufficiently repressive to keep prices from rising may be exceedingly costly in terms of lost output and social demoralization. At the least, one ought to be meticulously explicit

It Can't Be Done

The view that there is some level of taxation above which any increase in tax rates is abortive, i.e., will fail to release resources for public use, is not in itself very interesting. The interesting question is: What is the critical level? Generally speaking, the sophisticated man's answer has been, "It depends." Indeed, on one view "the elements of taxable capacity prove on closer investigation to be so contingent, subjective, and variable—to be so much a matter of circumstances of time and place, of institutional arrangements, and public attitudes—that they defy generalization, and any conclusion expressed in absolute or final terms is bound to misrepresent the very nature of the problem itself."[6]

Yet this is not the view of all sophisticated men. The nineteenth century English economist Bastable thought 15 per cent of national income about all that could be managed, and, more recently, Colin Clark has argued that to levy taxes in excess of 25-27 per cent of the national income is to court inflation no matter what use is made of the proceeds, and irrespective, apparently, not only of the level of income, the nature of the tax, and of central bank monetary measures, but also of taxpayers' habits of compliance and the government's administrative competence.[7]

If Clark had set the threshold at, say, 60 per cent, his proposition would hardly warrant comment. What makes 25 per cent

---

in weighing the social costs of alternative policies, and persistent and imaginative in exploring alternative means of cure. (All this, however, is once again largely a matter of cost-push.)

[6] Monteath Douglas, "Taxable Capacity and British and Canadian Experience," in *Limits of Taxable Capacity,* Tax Institute, Inc., 1953, p. 31.

[7] For references and an example of Clark's work, see *Limits of Taxable Capacity,* pp. 141 and 183.

(or 30 per cent) interesting is that not only in many western European countries but also in the United States the ratio of tax revenue to net national income, or even to GNP, has in fact been near or above 25 per cent throughout the postwar decade. Whatever one may think about the plausibility of a single, universal upper limit, it is important to know what truth there is to the 25-30 per cent contention in the particular setting of the United States of the late 1950's. Are we really at the end of the line?

The little evidence we have appears to be against Clark. Whether one uses the consumer price index or that for wholesale prices, whether concurrent data or a two- or three-year lag (as specified by Clark), whether 25 per cent or 27 per cent (or even 30 per cent), the only two periods since the war during which prices did not rise (1948-1949 and, depending on the index, 1951-1953 or 1954-1955) should have been, by Clark's conjecture, years of marked inflation. Evidently a ratio of tax revenue to national income in excess of 25 per cent (or 27 per cent, or 30 per cent) does not imply inflation.[8]

[8] We have often suffered price inflation in periods when the tax take was nowhere near 25 per cent of national income. But the crucial question is not whether inflation implies "25 per cent" but whether or not "25 per cent—plus" implies inflation. (I have taken Clark literally and used national income in the denominator. Perhaps he meant GNP; if so, the United States evidence is less conclusive, since the postwar ratio of taxes to GNP was below 27 per cent until 1956. Less conclusive, that is, as regards some of Clark's more eclectic formulations, which place the upper limit between 23 per cent and 27 per cent. If he means 25 per cent [and is willing to accept either the consumer or the wholesale index], part of the evidence is still relevant—and inconsistent with the hypothesis. [The implicit deflator for GNP fell only between 1948 and 1949. For sources, see note 1, p. 43.]

It is worth noting that since he first proposed 25 per cent as the limit, Clark has shifted his ground. In his early writing he based his position on political attitudes: on a presumption that as taxes approached 25 per cent of national income, important groups would shift their loyalties to inflation as a means of mitigating the burden. But if this is the mechanism, it is of the "it won't be done" variety. It implies

But whatever the historical facts, is it likely that increasing tax rates should be abortive, not to say inflationary, for revenue levels (or ratios to GNP) even substantially above those current in the United States? Note that the issue is not whether a $1 increase in taxes will suffice to release a full dollar's worth of resources for government use. Indeed, it can be shown that balancing extra expenditure by an *equal* amount of extra revenue is not likely to do the job; generally a $1 increase in taxes will induce less than a $1 cut in private spending. But to hold that it is impossible to increase public purchases without inflation is to hold that an increase in tax rates will release no more than *zero* cents' worth of resources. It is to hold that a rate increase would fail to reduce private spending by a penny—or, worse, that it would reduce the *supply* of goods and services by more than it would reduce private spending. Is this likely in the American setting for any feasible structure of taxes and irrespective of central bank action to make money tight?[9]

Those who, like Clark, think yes—who think that it is impossible, or nearly so, to release resources for public use without inflation by means of higher taxes—base their case on the incentive effects of taxes on the supply and allocation of "effort," on business spending on current account, and on the supply of risk capital. They argue, for instance, that a tax on income, by reducing the post-tax rate of ("take home") pay, is bound to cause a reduction in the supply of work. Taxes on

---

not that taxes and monetary measures are impotent to contain the price level, but that at or above 25 per cent enough influential people will prefer some inflation to fiscal and monetary stringency to carry the day—that elective politicians will be unwilling to raise taxes high enough to contain inflation.

[9] The "feasible" is not meant as a dodge. I have in mind conventional and generally accepted taxes which are administratively workable and the impact of which on distribution is politically acceptable.

profits, in turn, are alleged to induce businessmen to increase their spending on current account, since "the government foots half the bill." The net effect, all in all, is to increase rather than decrease any inflationary excess of demand over supply.[10]

It would be inappropriate here to rebut this view in full. Suffice it only to point out that not only is the empirical evidence about the effects of taxes on incentives all against the pessimists but also that their conclusion does not follow even if one grants the quantitative importance of the incentive effects on which they rest their case. To illustrate:

The pessimists' argument about the supply of effort hinges on the "substitution effect" of taxes. "Substitution effect" is the economist's label for the shift in demand, e.g., between tea and coffee, that occurs in response to a change in the relative prices of tea and coffee *with income held constant*. It is relevant, because a tax on, say, personal income reduces the "price" one has to pay in forgone earnings for working less, i.e., the price of "leisure," and thereby weakens the incentive to full-time work (for pay), to taking a part-time job on the side, or to accepting an offer of a more onerous but better paid job. By tending to reduce the supply and productivity of labor, all these effects tend to reduce the capacity supply of goods and services.

But "tend to" is used advisedly; the response of an individual to a change in what he collects for an hour of work will not depend on the substitution effect alone. The change will affect his income position, and the "income effect" works the other way. Just as a fall in income is likely to reduce one's "consumption" of operas, though the price of admission remains unchanged, it is likely to cause a reduction in one's consumption of leisure. The income effect of a personal income tax, or of a sales tax which is reflected in higher goods' prices, will incline

[10] A fourth effect often invoked has to do with the structure of costs, especially wage costs. Since this is primarily relevant to cost-push inflation, I defer comment to the Appendix.

people to work harder and longer, if not to maintain their prior income position, at least to limit the loss. (The strength of the income effect will vary, of course, with people's incomes and assets, and with the magnitude and flexibility of their financial obligations.)

In terms of these broad qualitative considerations, then, the effect of income taxes on the supply of effort is indeterminate. To establish a presumption one way or the other, one must look at the evidence—the more so since any number of nonpecuniary factors of motivation and institutional practice will influence the quantitative outcome (e.g., the simple fact that in most jobs one is not free to change hours of work, or the not-so-simple fact that considerations of power, status, and the like appear to weigh heavily in the calculations of professional people and executives). As regards the United States (and, more surprisingly, the United Kingdom) the available evidence is reassuring. While complaints and anecdotes purporting to illustrate drastic disincentive effects are plentiful, and systematic and disinterested research rather scarce, what there is of the latter suggests, in the words of a recent study for the Joint Economic Committee of the Congress, that "neither in Great Britain nor in the United States is there any convincing evidence that current high levels of taxation are seriously interfering with work incentives. There are, in fact . . . a number of good reasons for believing that considerably higher taxes could be sustained without injury to worker motivation should the need arise."[11]

[11] G. F. Break, "The Effects of Taxation on Work Incentives" in *Federal Tax Policy for Economic Growth and Stability,* Joint Committee on Economic Report, G.P.O., 1955, p. 199. See also the papers by Peter Henle, Clarence D. Long, and Crawford H. Greenewalt in the same volume. For other work on incentives and for references, see also G. F. Break, "Income Tax and Incentives to Work: An Empirical Study," *American Economic Review,* September 1957, and "Income Taxes, Wage Rates and Incentives to Supply Labor Services," *National Tax Journal,* December 1953; and T. H. Sanders, *Effects of Taxation on*

But what if it were otherwise—if a tax increase were likely to cause an appreciable decline in the supply of labor and hence in capacity output? To sustain the "can't be done" position—the position that taxes are impotent to release additional resources for public use—that is not enough. For a tax increase to be abortive, *the tax-induced decline in capacity output must be larger than the tax-induced reduction in private spending.* A simple arithmetical example will show what is involved:

Assume that, from an initial situation of no tax, there is levied an income tax with an average yield of 30 per cent and a marginal yield of 50 per cent on a man whose taxable net income, all earned, is $10,000. Assume also that this person will reduce his consumption spending by as little as, say, 60 cents for each $1 decline in his disposable income (cutting his rate of saving by 40 cents). If he sticks to his pre-tax work habits, the tax will reduce his disposable income by $3,000, inducing a $1,200 drop in his annual rate of saving and a $1,800 cut in consumption. The $1,800 measures the volume of resources that would be released for public use.[12]

What if he decided to take it a little easier, to cut down on hours of work or shift to a less onerous occupation? This would certainly reduce the resource-releasing effect of the tax. But as a little arithmetic will show, for the effect to vanish, i.e., for the tax to become abortive, the taxpayer in question would have to reduce his work output by 25.7 per cent and his disposable income by *42 per cent or more.* He would have to accept a cut of at least $4,285 in his post-tax income (from $10,000 to $5,715)—$2,570 due to less work and $1,715 to satisfy the tax collector. This would imply a $2,570 cut in his

---

Executives (Boston: Harvard University Graduate School of Business Administration), 1951.

[12] To simplify the arithmetic I assume that our taxpayer's gross income equals his net income.

spending for consumption, i.e., a cut in demand which matched exactly the drop in his work output, and thus would leave the *balance* between supply and demand unchanged. It would imply, also, a reduction of $1,715 per year in his saving.[13]

One need not belabor the point. There is no evidence to suggest that in the aggregate the (negative) substitution effect will exceed the (positive) income effect even on supply. Moreover, the pessimist view that the resource-releasing potential of income taxes is nil ignores the income effect on *demand,* which, after all, is the excuse for levying the tax to start off with. According to the best econometric estimates, a one billion dollar increase in revenues, raised by an across-the-board 3 per cent increase in all federal income tax rates, would reduce consumption by approximately three-quarters of a billion dollars. There exists no good theoretical or empirical reason to think that such a cut in spending would be neutralized by a reduction in the supply of effort.[14]

[13] If initially he was saving less than $1,715 per annum, i.e., less than 17 per cent of his income, he would either have to borrow and/or use up past savings to keep the cut in consumption to $2,570, or reduce consumption even more (i.e., by more than 60 per cent of the decline in post-tax income). If the latter—and there are not many who can afford the former—it would take an even larger cut in his income-earning work for the resource-releasing effect to shrink to zero.

All this, of course, is sensitive to the particular structure of the tax in question and to the effect on consumption of a decline in disposable income. In general, the larger the cut in consumption induced by a given decline in disposable income, the smaller the marginal rate of the tax, and the larger the average rate, the greater does the drop in output have to be to make the tax abortive. (With given average rates, low marginal rates are likely also to have less deleterious effect on effort, i.e., to induce less substitution of leisure for work, than high marginal rates. In contrast, the higher the average rate [the ratio of tax-take to income] the more important the work-inducing income effect is likely to become; the extra bit of income matters more, the greater the tax-bite.)

[14] Always assuming, of course, that public *demand* takes the place of private. For a report on the calculation, see Musgrave, "The Incidence of the Tax Structure," in *Federal Tax Policy,* p. 104. (*Cont'd.*)

All this is safe enough if one is allowed some choice among taxes and leeway to tighten up on money. But what if we should be restricted to very "progressive" taxes, so called, e.g., taxes on profits, on unearned incomes, and on high-bracket earned incomes? It is these which are supposed to be weak in reducing consumption spending, to stimulate wasteful corporate spending on current account, and to discourage risk capital.

As to the impact of progressiveness as such, the evidence is not clear. While the rich spend on consumption a much smaller fraction of their income than do the poor, the *marginal* ratio, i.e., the incremental *change* in consumption due to a *change* in post-tax income, does not appear to vary greatly with income except at the quantitatively insignificant poles of the income spectrum. And for our purposes it is this last, the "*marginal* propensity-to-consume," that matters.

But quite apart from progressiveness, we know little about the impact of the corporate income tax; it is not at all clear who pays how much of it, as between the stockholder (in reduced corporate earnings) and the consumer (in higher prices, hence in reduced real income). To the extent that the tax is "pushed forward" in the form of price increases (or back on to wage earners)—it has been estimated that about one-third of the burden is so passed on[15]—a corporate tax is much like a sales

---

For the sake of symmetry, mention should be made of the substitution effect of the income tax on *spending*. Qualitatively, an increase in income tax rates will cause the sensitive and calculating income earner to reallocate in favor of current consumption and against saving, since the tax, if it is expected to continue, reduces the future post-tax income to be expected as a reward for thrift. Quantitatively, however, the effect appears to be negligible as concerns our standard taxes; as regards consumption, at least, it is the income effect that counts (cf. Musgrave). (There would be a far from negligible reverse effect, of course, if instead of taxing income we taxed consumption via high excise taxes or a spending tax.)

[15] Cf. Musgrave, *op. cit.*, p. 100.

tax (or income tax) and is neither progressive nor for other reasons weak in its effect on consumption. But to the extent that corporations absorb the tax, not by reducing dividends (in which case the income effect is akin to that of a progressive income tax) but by running down retained earnings, the induced cut in consumption will be small.[16]

On the other hand, even that portion of the tax which is so absorbed may have, via liquidity and rate-of-return calculations, a resource-releasing effect on *investment*. The widely held notion that such negative effects on investment are not anti-inflationary is mistaken; investment expenditure constitutes demand for currently produced goods and services no less than consumption expenditure. That in six months or a year (or two) investment gives rise to additional capacity does not alter the fact that in bidding for today's or this year's supply of scarce resources it competes with consumption spending and government spending. (It is a different matter that a diversion of resources from private investment to private or public consumption—but not public *investment*—will increase current consumption at the expense of potential future consumption; whether or not that is desirable is an issue of resource allocation and not of current inflation control.)[17]

What of the oft-cited substitution effect of the corporate in-

[16] An increase in prices just large enough to pay the extra tax, i.e., an increase the proceeds of which do not accrue as extra wage or profit income to private spenders, constitutes a limited ("one-round") cost-push which, however, helps to release resources from private use and to contain "demand-pull." For comment, see the Appendix.

[17] Even if investment resulted *instantaneously* in ready-to-operate capacity, i.e., if it took no time to build plants and machines, $1 of investment in, say, plant or equipment (not to speak of dams and roads) would add much more to current demand than to current supply. In the United States it takes on the average about $1.50+ of investment to increase *annual* manufacturing capacity by $1. (In steel, to take a suggestive case, it takes over 2 tons of steel, let alone labor and other inputs, to increase annual capacity by 1 ton; two years of a new mill's capacity production goes into replacing the steel that was used up in its own construction.)

come tax on business purse strings? No doubt, taxes on profit render liberal expense accounts and various expensable projects less costly: the Treasury pays some of the bill. And to the extent that such "expenses" are not genuine costs of current production, but consumption by executives or salesmen, or investment, they do absorb some "final" output. Again, however, there is a countervailing income effect. It is true that with a 52 per cent marginal rate, 52 cents of a dollar of expense is "free." But the tax happens also to reduce total profit, and it may be that even a 48-cent expense item that is not really necessary is too much out of already shrunken profits. A $200 theater party at a $100,000 profit level may hurt less than $100 for the same party from a $50,000 profit base.

All in all, neither qualitative reasoning nor quantitative evidence provides any support for the claim, as concerns the United States, that it is impossible without creating an inflationary gap to release additional resources for public use by means of the conventional instruments of the Treasury and the Federal Reserve. Government spending, while it contributed to the recurrent postwar excess of total demand, need not have caused inflation; the inflationary effect of federal as of state-local spending could have been offset by more resolute use of taxes and of the monetary powers of the Federal Reserve. The view that an increase in tax rates, if accompanied by tight money, would have been impotent to reduce private spending and eliminate the excess is untenable.[18]

[18] This is not to deny the strategic and tactical difficulties of operating an effective stabilization policy—one that will maintain a fine balance between spending and capacity. Matters of timing and magnitude are delicate, forecasting is very much an art, and the machinery of administration and legislation cumbersome; hence the best we can hope for is to cut down substantially on the amounts by which we miss. The burden of the above is only that the difficulties are not qualitatively greater and may in fact be less great in a high-G economy than in a low-G economy. (For the bearing on all the above of cost-push inflation, see the Appendix.)

There remains, however, still another line of argument which links public spending, if only implicitly, with inflation. Granted that "won't be done" is for our purposes irrelevant, and "can't be done" plain wrong, what of "shouldn't be done" —of the view that the level of taxation required to offset the postwar volume of public spending would have been too high to bear?

It Shouldn't Be Done

The major premise of the "shouldn't be done" thesis is that "*can* be done" too is irrelevant, that "the test of a critical point measured by reference to inflationary consequences, even when all variable circumstances of time and place are allowed for, is not a satisfactory criterion because more immediate limiting factors are likely to make themselves felt before the anti-inflationary effect of taxation is exhausted." The minor premise, in turn, consists in an empirical judgment: "Taxation, in fact, has . . . reached levels where it has begun to involve non-financial and social costs of a more or less incalculable order." The customary moral, that we must reduce taxes and hence cut public spending, is assumed inexorably to follow. But does it?[19]

---

[19] The alternative conclusion, that taxes should be reduced but spending maintained, is not often heard except during periods of recession and depression, when substantial resources are idle. As a device for releasing resources for public use, inflation can, of course, serve as a substitute for taxes, but few would argue that it is preferable to suffering the side effects of taxes. In public discussion, at least, the argument invariably ends up as in the text above. (The quotations are from Douglas in *Taxable Capacity, op. cit.*, pp. 32 and 34. It should be said that Douglas is not a proponent of the "customary moral." His essay is a most intelligent and sophisticated treatment of the issue of taxable capacity, and I quote him not because I disagree with him, as I do in part, about where his argument leads, but because the cited passages, taken out of context, provide a conveniently succinct point of departure.)

The major premise is solid enough. Our failure during World War II to maintain the budget on a "pay as you go" basis, i.e., to raise taxes and make money sufficiently tight to release 45 per cent of GNP for public use, reflected concern not with the impotence of taxes but rather with possible side effects on incentives and on the distribution of scarce necessities.[20] Resort to the paraphernalia of price control and rationing made sense not because inflation could not have been contained by higher taxes (and really tight money) but because such taxes might well have impeded the mobilization effort and been unfair in their incidence in terms of widely held notions of equity. (It does not follow that we were wise not to use the fisc more aggressively than we did.)

Nor can one quarrel with the minor premise if interpreted literally. The nonfinancial and social costs of current levels of taxation are indeed difficult to calculate. But it is an odd argument which leads from uncertain knowledge to certain conclusions. What "incalculable" is evidently meant to mean is not that the side effects are impossible to gauge but that on calculation they appear to be significantly large, in fact too large to bear.

Suspending judgment about whether as a matter of logic the conclusion is really implied by the premises, what are these "incalculable" costs of taxation which appear to loom so large on the American scene? If one searches the arguments of the less sophisticated, it turns out that many of the supposedly dangerous side effects are not *side* effects at all. People who worry because taxes reduce investment, or weigh heavily on consumption, or take away income from some people to give it to others, are not worried about the side effects of taxes. They are unhappy about the very reallocation of resources from private to public use, or that redistribution of command over

[20] "Pay as you go" would not, in fact, have done the job; we would have had to run a substantial cash surplus.

resources, which it is the function of taxes to facilitate. They may or may not be right, but the issue is hardly one of side effects. It is, in fact, the paramount issue of economic choice: how to allocate scarce resources between alternative uses and among different people.[21]

Taxes do, of course, have some genuinely side effects. They give rise to inefficiencies in resource use which benefit no one. (The above discussed substitution effects on effort are of this sort.) Also, they leave their mark on social and political institutions and behavior, and thereby touch on many non-economic values. But, even if we grant that such effects are appreciable and damaging, the conclusion that we must reduce taxes and public spending simply does not follow. It is not enough to demonstrate the existence of damaging side effects. For judgment about the level of spending, those effects must be weighed against the differential benefits and costs of the public activities which taxes make possible, i.e., against the *primary* consequences of taxing and spending—for resource allocation and distribution, and for political institutions. It is to these primary consequences we now turn.[22]

[21] The following is a typical example of how value judgments about allocation and distribution tend to slip into the argument: "Corporation taxes may now take as much as 70 per cent of a corporation's income. Short of total war, they have never been so high. They take away funds that *should* be reinvested to buy new plant and equipment for growing enterprises and they lower the dividends the stockholders *should fairly* receive." (C. L. Turner, "Presidential Address," Tax Institute, *Taxable Capacity,* p. 55; the italics are mine.)

[22] Even if one were to conclude that the evil effects of the last $3 billion of taxes outweigh the differential benefits which associate with the public use of the tax-released resources, it still does not follow that expenditure should be cut. There is no higher ordinance forbidding other courses of action, e.g., giving way to some price inflation or using direct controls. The conclusion that these choices are even less acceptable must rest on a careful matching of their consequences against those of reducing public services. There is no basis for an a priori presumption that, e.g., 2 per cent inflation per annum is necessarily the worst of all evils. In fact, it is surely not.

5 THE ALLOCATION OF SCARCE RESOURCES (1)

Have We Skimped on Private Shares?

It is the contention of the previous chapter that the goal of avoiding inflation provides little or no guidance to the appropriate balance between public and private spending. As a society, we are within wide limits free to choose how much of our substance to devote to "public" as against private purposes, and free also, by vigorous exercise of the fiscal and monetary powers of government, to make good on the choice without resort either to inflation or to direct controls. The twin goals of full employment (more or less) and price stability provide a target for the *total* level of spending for goods and services but leave the public-private balance undetermined.[1]

What then is involved in choosing the level of government spending? What is the measure of "excess"? One of the odd things about the postwar debate is that it tends to evade what is in a sense the central economic issue: choice among alternative uses for scarce resources. Public purchase of goods and services absorbs labor, plant, machinery, materials, etc., and

[1] The fact that in a world of cost-push there may be no "target" that will fully satisfy both goals, and that "hitting" a given target is a difficult business, in no sense affects the conclusion. Cost-push difficulties, and those of operating an effective stabilization policy, will be with us whether government takes 5 per cent or 25 per cent of GNP.

hence reduces what is available for production on private account. More for G implies less for personal consumption (C) and private investment (I); in fact, the measure of the economic burden is precisely the C and I which the community must forgo to have the G. The assertion, then, that government spending on goods and services has been excessive implies that we have had too much of defense, postal services, hospital construction, and the like, as against consumer goods, residential construction, or private plant and equipment. It implies that we have stinted personal consumption and private investment to splurge on G.

Have we skimped on the private shares? There is no objective answer—no answer that is independent of a complex of social and private values. There exists no "test of necessity," no self-evident indicator of essential needs and inessential wants acceptable to all people of sound judgment. It does not follow, however, that we are reduced to a catalogue of unchallengeable assertions based on personal preference. At the least, it is possible to set some limits to legitimate contention by spelling out the facts about allocation. The simple discipline of confronting every claim that we are doing too much of this or too little of that with the quantitative facts of what we are doing and the quantitative implications of the prescription has surprising therapeutic value. More than this, it is useful to test actual allocations against rather general and widely held goals, e.g., the goal that over time consumption per head should keep rising. Such testing cannot in itself prove that we have misallocated, but, if it should reveal substantial gaps between performance and objectives, it would serve to warn us that something may be amiss, that we had better reconsider.

It is the aim of this chapter to search the gross statistical indicators of our postwar economic performance for such warnings. Does the evidence warrant a presumption that we have stinted on consumption or private investment in terms of widely held values? More modestly, what are the facts on which a presumption would have to be based?

Personal Consumption (C)

"Onward and upward" is an important goal for most Americans; most of us believe that our standard of living should keep rising. Strictly speaking, this need not imply that the level of *personal* consumption need rise—roads, municipal swimming pools and clinics, and the portion of income added to savings also matter—but for most of us it implies just that. Allocation that fails to provide for increasing personal consumption is suspect.[2]

The relevant statistics, those on total, per capita, and per household consumption, all measured in terms of the 1957 level of prices, are given in Table 15.[3] The critical series, that on "real" per capita consumption (C^*/P), is at least moderately reassuring. With a rise from $1,091 in 1929 and $1,413 in 1947 to $1,631 in 1957, it is evident that C^* per head has shown a rising trend. Everyone's consumption could have increased, even if not everyone's did, without a cut in government purchases and in private investment. The share of productive capacity available to produce for consumption has been

[2] Of course, consumption could fail to rise, indeed could fall, as between 1929 and 1932, not because G and I take more than a "fair" share but because of failure to maintain *total* spending ($C + I + G$), and hence incomes, high enough to make full use of the productive capacity of the economy. When that happens, i.e., in recession or depression, falling consumption must not be blamed on an excess of G. The opposite is closer to the truth. Only in periods of more or less full employment and full utilization does more for G and I imply less for C, and hence it is the level of C in such periods of full employment that we must examine. For our present purposes the figures for the 1930's, 1949, and 1953-1954 are irrelevant.

[3] The table also contains series on the ratio of consumption to GNP and to "civilian" GNP. (Recall that P stands for population, 1947-1957 for fiscal years unless otherwise indicated, and that the asterisk denotes adjustment to fiscal 1957 prices.)

sufficient to satisfy, in direction if not in magnitude, the "onward and upward" goal.[4]

A slow rise in a level of consumption so low as to violate one's sense of a decent minimum would not, of course, be of much comfort. Whether the recent United States levels are, in this sense, "low," everyone must judge for himself—everyone,

[4] The fact that not everyone's consumption did increase implies redistribution effects which are quite another matter. The point here is that G* and I* did not pre-empt so much capacity as to preclude a rise in everyone's personal consumption. On the other hand, the share of C in GNP declined from 75.6 per cent in 1929 to 64.1 per cent in 1957, with a low of 52 per cent in 1944, a postwar low of 63.1 per cent in 1952, and a postwar high of 70.6 per cent in 1947 (Column 5, Table 15). As a fraction of nondefense GNP, C fell from 76.1 per cent in 1929 to 71.5 per cent in 1957, with the postwar peak at 75.4 per cent (1947) and most postwar years between 72 and 75 per cent. Between fiscal 1947 and 1957, C* grew at a compound annual rate of 3.21 per cent and population at 1.74 per cent.

It is worth noting, incidentally, that the above dollar figures of per capita consumption make no allowance for increase in the consumption of that important commodity, leisure. Average weekly hours worked in manufacturing, for instance, declined from 44.2 in 1929 to 40.5 in prosperous 1956. (For all activities taken together the decline between 1929 and 1956 was close to eight hours.) With net spendable weekly earnings (i.e., earnings less social security and income taxes) in manufacturing for workers with no dependents at $68.04 and for workers with three dependents at $75.64, the weekly four-hour increase in leisure represents about $350 worth of "consumption" per worker per year. (Paid vacations per worker in 1956 averaged a little over a week.)

Other interesting information on the rise in real consumption is implied by the following facts about electrical appliances: between 1946 and 1956 the proportion of "wired homes" with refrigerators increased from 69.1 per cent to 96 per cent; those with freezers from 4.3 per cent (1948) to 18 per cent; those with vacuum cleaners from 48.8 per cent to 66.7 per cent; those with electrical washers from 60.5 per cent to 86.8 per cent; and those with TV sets, if that be progress, from 2.9 per cent (1948) to 81 per cent. During the same ten-year period, the number of "wired homes" increased from 31 million to 47 million. The proportion of families owning automobiles, in turn, rose from 54 per cent in 1948 to 73 per cent in 1956. (*Economic Report of the President*, 1957, G.P.O., p. 111.)

that is, inclined to judging policy. With disposable income (personal income after taxes and transfers) in 1957 at $6,035 per household and average household consumption at $5,593; with purchases of nondurables and services running at $4,801 per household, and of consumer durables at $791; with residential construction at a rate of $348 per household, my reaction, I must admit, is one of complacency. I fail to see that the squeeze on personal consumption justifies an attack on G, or on civilian G and FG (at $803 and $98 per household in fiscal 1957)—that we should cut back on defense, or on education, or on urban renewal, or on hospital-building, simply in order to use more of our substance for personal consumption.[5, 6]

[5] On the other hand, I would not hold that a household consumption level of $5,600 is enough for bliss, that a sensible man should not care about having personal consumption rise further. Moreover, while I find the average comforting, I do not think that we can afford to be complacent about the distribution of consumption. Not that I have an absolute objection to inequality—above a certain level, and within limits, I object more both to the measures that would be required to eliminate it and also to some likely consequences of "equality" as such. But it is only too evident that a great many people in the United States still live, and a great many children are still brought up, at a level below anything like a decent minimum. Indeed, if I thought that the best way to eliminate the remaining pockets of primitive poverty would be to release more resources for conventional personal consumption, I would be less comfortable about the level of C (and hence of G and I), irrespective of the average. But it happens that the most effective means for overcoming such poverty (e.g., public health measures; provision of cheap power, decent housing, and irrigation and extension services; improvement of education; tax concessions and other subsidies to encourage private industrial development) generally involve not only more public nonexhaustive spending but also more G.

[6] The cited figures are based on the Census Bureau's definition of "household," which includes all persons who share "a dwelling unit, that is a house, an apartment or other group of rooms, or a room that constitutes 'separate living quarters.'" (*Statistical Abstract,* 1958, p. 2.) After making the calculations I discovered that the Office of Business Economics has a more restrictive series on "families and unattached individuals" (*Income and Output,* p. 161), of which there

But this is one man's judgment; everyone must make up his own mind. What stands is the need, if prescription is to be honest, for attention to the facts and for explicit value judgments. It is a need not often satisfied in our public discussions.

Private Investment (I)

What about private capital formation? Have we shortchanged I in favor of C and G? Striking a balance between consumption, whether private or public, and investment is a subtle business—more so than choosing among various kinds of consumption. It involves choice between the present and the future—indeed, partial commitment to a particular kind of future. Moreover, it is not easy to identify widely held values against which to test how we have done. Nonetheless it is worth looking at the facts, if only to discipline prescription.

Table 16 contains the relevant information for 1929-1957. It appears that the postwar share of gross private domestic investment in GNP has varied between 13.1 per cent in 1954 (a recession year) and 18.6 per cent in 1951, with, to take only periods of full employment, 1947 at 13.5 per cent, 1948 at 15.1 per cent, 1952 at 15.2 per cent, 1955 at 14.7 per cent, 1956 at 16.4 per cent, and 1957 at 15.6 per cent. These compare with a ratio of 15.5 per cent in 1929, and with postdepression figures of 13.1 per cent in 1940 and 14.4 per cent in 1941. As regards the share of gross private investment in total output, at least, there has been no significant change between 1929 and the years since the war.[7]

---

were some 53.15 million in fiscal 1957, as compared to the 49.5 million in the Census household series (Table 3). On a "per family" basis, post-tax income in Fiscal 1957 was $5,621, consumption was $5,209 (of which $737 went on durables), and residential construction per family came to $325.

[7] In periods of recession investment generally declines more than GNP; hence the ratios are lower. For instance, in 1932 the ratio was

If one takes only producers' fixed investment, eliminating inventory accumulation and residential construction, the qualitative result is the same. The 1929 ratio to GNP of 10.5 per cent compares with 1947-1957 figures which range from 9.5 per cent to 10.8 per cent, with six of the eleven years above 10 per cent. (The post-depression high, in 1940, was 8 per cent.) The ratio of producers' fixed investment to nondefense GNP, in turn, exceeded 11 per cent in eight of the first eleven postwar years, with 1957 at 12.1 per cent, as compared with 10.5 per cent in 1929.

None of this implies that the volume of resources allotted to private investment has been in some sense sufficient. There is nothing sacrosanct about the 1929 ratio, or any ratio for that matter. What the facts do suggest, however, is that we have not done any worse by private investment since 1947 than we did in the last pre-New Deal year of prosperity.[8]

There are also other tests we can apply. Investment is important not because we care about turret lathes and refineries but because adding to and replacing old plant and machinery increase the capacity of the economy to produce things we do care about. If the rate of investment had been so low as to

---

1.5 per cent. But this must not be blamed on an excess of C and G. With GNP* (= C* + I* + G*) in 1932 some $55 billion below its 1929 level, i.e., 29 per cent below the demonstrated capacity of the economy in 1929, we could have had a lot more of everything

[8] This does raise the question of how prosperous 1929 really was. Judging by the Kendrick-National Bureau series for pre-1929 GNP* ("Commerce concept"), real national product in 1929 was about 6 per cent higher than in 1928. Moreover, while Barger's figures (in *Outlay and Income in the U.S., 1921-1938,* National Bureau of Economic Research, 1942) suggest a decline in total spending between the second and fourth quarters of 1929, the relative share of gross private investment appears actually to have risen (in part, no doubt, as a consequence of unintended inventory accumulation). (For the Kendrick series, see Vol. II, p. A-104 in *Productivity Trends in the U.S.,* National Bureau of Economic Research [forthcoming].)

keep capacity-GNP* from rising, or from rising faster than population, most of us would, I think, be concerned. Indeed, one might be inclined to worry if the postwar rise in capacity output had been any slower than the rate of advance before, say, 1929. It turns out, however, that we have done if anything a little better since 1947 than we did in the "good old days." Between (calendar) 1947 and 1956 (to take years of capacity operation) GNP* increased at an average compound rate of 4.01 per cent per year, as against 3.70 per cent between 1889 and 1929, 3.48 per cent in the 1920's (1919-1929), and a long-term trend rate, since 1839, of about 3.5 per cent. On a per capita basis, the 1947-1956 rate of growth was 2.25 per cent, well above the 1889-1929 rate of 1.96 per cent, and higher also than the 1839-1959 trend-rate of 1.75 per cent.[9]

If the postwar acceleration had been due to faster growth of the labor force (relative to population), i.e., to more people doing more hours of work, the gain over pre-1929 growth-rates

[9] The average rate of growth between (calendar) 1947 and 1957, at 3.69 per cent, was substantially lower than the 1947-1956 average, but it tells us nothing about capacity growth. Both 1957 and 1958 show the effect of the recession: actual GNP* was well below capacity-GNP* in both years. Nonetheless, the record from early 1956 on is less reassuring. The rise in GNP* between calendar 1955 and calendar 1956 was only 2.4 per cent, while during 1956 itself the rate of growth was down to about 1.4 per cent. It is difficult to judge from aggregate data how much of the slowdown was due to a deceleration in capacity growth and how much to a pre-recession deceleration in demand; price indices don't help much. Judging by the early 1959 figures, I doubt if there is much cause for worry; but we won't really know whether we are back on the postwar trend until the figures for the first half of 1960 are in. (The growth-rate calculations for 1889-1929 were made by using the figures for 1889, 1919, and 1929 from the Kendrick-National Bureau series on GNP in 1929 prices ["Commerce concept"] and the population series given in *Historical Statistics of the United States*. The 1947-1956 rates are based on the Commerce Department's GNP series, converted to 1929 dollars. The long-term trend rates are those calculated by Raymond Goldsmith; they cover the period 1839-1959. [For a report of the calculations see *Historical and Comparative Rates of Production,* Part 2 of *Hearings,* April 1959, Joint Economic Committee, U. S. Congress, G.P.O., 1959.])

would not be particularly pleasing. But that is not the case. Since 1947 labor productivity has also increased faster, at least on the average, than before 1929: between 1889 and 1929 real output per man-hour increased at an average annual rate of 2.04 per cent; the 1947-1956 rate was 3.5 per cent. Investment cannot be credited for all or even most of this, of course; much of the increase in labor productivity is due to improvements in technology, management, labor skills, etc., rather than to a growing stock of capital. But that is beside the point. The important fact for our purposes is that private investment in the postwar period has been sufficient to permit real capacity output, output per capita, and output per man-hour to grow faster than before 1929.[10]

The basic question—how should we balance off the present against the future—remains, of course, wide open. Is a 4 per cent rate of growth about right, or should we try for 5 per cent? Surveying our "needs" for defense, urban renewal, medical facilities, education, and the like, the recent Rockefeller Broth-

[10] It is exceedingly difficult to sort out the effects of changes in technology from the effects of increases in capital; new machines embody a different technology from that of old machines. In a world of technological change the very notion of *net* investment is fuzzy. When an old, worn-out, manually operated machine is replaced by a brand new automatic, how much of the cost of the latter represents replacement and how much net addition to the stock of capital? If one is interested in the effect of investment on capacity, then neither historical-cost nor replacement-cost depreciation is an adequate measure of pure "replacement." It can be shown, in fact, that replacement-cost depreciation on a straight-line basis substantially overstates what it would take to "maintain" current capacity intact. (The productivity computations are based on Kendrick's series on real gross product and unweighted man-hours for the private domestic economy, as given in Fabricant, *Basic Facts on Productivity Change,* Occasional Paper 63, National Bureau of Economic Research, 1959, pp. 42ff. The computations are for "private" product only, i.e., exclude value added by government. The value of "inputs" purchased by government is the only measure we have of government "output"; there exists no good independent measure that could be matched against the labor-hours devoted to governmental activity.)

ers Fund report concluded that "a 4 per cent rate of growth would enable us to meet all the low-estimate demands for government expenditure outlined in [their] Report, cover the capital investment requirements, and give a growth in the annual rate of consumer expenditures equal to the recent past."[11] But 4 per cent would barely do; the authors of the report would like to see us try for 5 per cent. The more cold-war minded, in turn, are apt to be uncomfortable about any rate of growth less than the Russian 6–7 per cent.[12]

It is not for us here to debate the merits of the case for or against 5 per cent or 6 per cent. Nor would I care to argue that we could achieve even a 5 per cent rate of growth without

[11] *The Challenge to America: Its Economic and Social Aspects,* Doubleday, 1958, p. 71.

[12] Apparently, their discomfort is not mitigated either by the fact that even with a 3 per cent differential it will take the Russians some time to match us in GNP* or per capita GNP*—that a 4 per cent increment to our GNP* still yields a larger absolute increase in output than does their 7 per cent applied to a GNP* about half of ours; or by the even more important fact that in a world of nuclear weapons the link between increases (above a certain level) in capacity-GNP*, on the one hand, and military strength on the other is much weaker than in the context of a World War II type situation. It is at least arguable that it is not necessarily dangerous that the Russian economy is growing somewhat faster than ours. If we "match" their military effort in absolute military terms and step up our aid to the underdeveloped countries—a double program of deterrence that should surely not be too difficult with a capacity-GNP* twice the size of the Russians'—the fact that they are beginning to approach levels of output which would permit a Western standard of life might have a mellowing effect on their political behavior. Countries where the standard of life is reasonably high and rising, where people acquire a stake in life as it is, are less likely to want to commit atomic suicide. At the least, as long as our nuclear and limited-war type retaliatory capability is in good order—a big if!—a prosperous and therefore increasingly bourgeois-minded Russia is not likely to become more destructive simply *on account of such prosperity.* (This is, of course, rather too crude a formulation of the case—I am aware of all the demonstration-effect arguments—but even on a much subtler level I think it as easy plausibly to defend the point as to attack it.)

a substantial shift of resources to investment. We almost certainly could not. But should we decide on a 5 per cent target, it does not follow that cutting G would be the only or even the best way to achieve the necessary reallocation to investment. For one thing, there is no presumption that the last billion dollars' worth of *public* consumption-type expenditure is necessarily of lower priority than the last billion dollars' worth of *personal* consumption spending (not even on grounds of strict "consumer sovereignty"). As a matter of fact, many programs of so-called public "consumption," e.g., those designed to improve health, sanitation, education, and technical training, etc., may well have a considerable effect on the productivity of the working population and hence be more appropriately labeled as "investment." Perhaps equally important, more than a third of G, as of nondefense G, consists of bona fide fixed investment; and it is quite possible that to shift resources from public investment in transport, power, research facilities, etc., into private investment in order to secure faster growth would be self-defeating.[13]

[13] In fact, one possible explanation of the increase since 1947 of the United States rate of growth is that the ratio to GNP of total gross investment, inclusive of public investment, has been almost certainly higher recently than it was in 1929, even with defense items excluded. In 1957, for instance, private producers' fixed investment made up 10.8 per cent and government fixed investment 6.4 per cent of GNP, for a total of 17.2 per cent. In 1929, private fixed-I came to 10.5 per cent, while *all* of G took 8.1 per cent. Unless, therefore, at least 82 per cent of G in 1929 was for *fixed* investment, the 1929 ratio of total producers' fixed investment to GNP was below the 1957 ratio. Taking nondefense magnitudes, public and private fixed-I in 1957 made up 2.9 per cent and 12.1 per cent of civilian GNP, for a total of 15 per cent. The 1929 rate could have been as high only if 60 per cent of all civilian G was for fixed investment. (On the other hand, the ratio of *net* to gross investment has fallen—more of I is for replacement.)

Incidentally, the United States all-investment figures since 1952 are most impressive. Even if one excludes investment in consumers' durables and inventory accumulation, the ratio of gross public plus private investment to GNP in 1957, for instance, was 21 per cent. With con-

But what if it were otherwise—if increasing the volume of private investment were the best way to speed up growth? Does it follow that we would have to reduce personal consumption or government purchases from their *current* full-employment levels? If capacity output were stationary, it certainly would. But capacity is far from stationary. At current levels of GNP even a 3 per cent rate of growth yields a yearly margin of some $14 billion; with a 4 per cent rate, the available increment is closer to $18 billion. Evidently it would be possible to maintain consumption and government expenditure at their current levels and yet raise the level of private investment by $14-$18 billion by the end of one year. Indeed, even if G and C were allowed to *increase* by 3–4 per cent each year, i.e., this next year by $3+ billion and $10 billion respectively, there would still be room for a 3–4 per cent annual increase in private investment —a rise over the next year of around $2.5 billion. Only if the required annual increase in private investment were to exceed 3–4 per cent of GNP (i.e., 19-20 per cent of I), would there have to be an absolute if temporary cut in C and/or G. And even then it is not axiomatic that the whole burden should fall on G. At least, it is not axiomatic *if we take seriously the doctrine that the proper end of economic activity is to cater to the individual consumer.*[14]

---

sumer durables included, the gross total exceeded 30 per cent of GNP. (While it would not do, in comparing our investment rate with that of, say, the Russians, to include all purchases of consumer durables, there is no doubt that some part of such "consumption" does constitute productive investment. E.g., the stock of private cars constitutes a substantial reservoir of future transport services, and even household freezers are an important means for economizing on resources used for food distribution. Think of what it would mean for transport facilities, and for wives and husbands too, if housewives had to shop daily.)

[14] Such back-of-the-envelope arithmetic in terms of gross aggregates is not designed, of course, to yield anything finer than first-approximation orders of magnitude. In particular, the feasibility of a rapid, large,

and disproportionate change, such as a 20 per cent increase within twelve months in the annual volume of investment, would have to be checked out in terms of a variety of specific kinds of capacity: steel, machine tools, and the like. But it must not be thought that reallocation problems render aggregative calculation invalid. The economy is capable of much more and faster conversion and substitution than most people assume. (It is curious how little faith some of the most passionate defenders of free enterprise seem to have in the efficacy of the price system in reallocating resources.)

It is sometimes argued that aggregative calculation is useless because fiscal and monetary measures are less than precise instruments of control. True, an effective stabilization strategy requires that one leave plenty of room for error, but the admitted danger of overshooting or undershooting does not void the need to fix on targets. Moreover, if overshooting be judged more damaging than leaving some capacity unused, the means to safety consists in a larger cushion of permanently maintained slack, not in cutting down the pace of advance.

6 THE ALLOCATION OF SCARCE RESOURCES (2)

Government and the Sovereign Consumer

To a Manchester liberal with iron in his soul, the above search of the statistics for warning symptoms of misallocation would very likely appear an irrelevant if not heretical exercise. On a strict laissez-faire view, to pose the question of the public-private balance in terms of where the extra $500 million might best go is to miss the crucial ethical issue: Is, or is not, the consumer to be sovereign? If we believe that the objective of economic activity is to cater to the individual consumer, then, it is argued, we must abide by the allocations implied by consumers' tastes as revealed by their market choices. Absorption of resources by paternalistic activities which do not meet a market "test" is prima facie illegitimate; and, while it must be tolerated as the lesser of evils as regards provision for defense, the administration of jails, and other "obviously" public activities, any shift of resources from private to public use is to be deplored irrespective of how much you and I may prefer more public hospitals to more automobiles. Or so the argument goes.

In fact, few people believe in the doctrine of consumer sovereignty in its pure, unadulterated form. But what if everyone did? What if we could all agree that consumers' preferences are the only admissible touchstone for economic performance

—that we will suppress any qualms about attributing ultimate significance to people's television-bombarded tastes for appliances (and disregard all difficulties with children and the insane and all problems of technical ignorance)? Would it follow that there is no need for allocating resources through political decision? Or does the very doctrine of consumer sovereignty impose on government, aside from its income distribution, stabilization, and general policing functions, an obligation partially to short-circuit market processes in the allocation of resources?[1]

A Digression on Market Efficiency

The negative contention—that there is no call for allocation by government—stands or falls with the crucial minor premise of the laissez-faire position, notably that a price-market system is such an efficient instrument for inducing consumers to reveal their preferences and producers to cater to these that allocations not subjected to a market test are bound to do worse by consumers than allocations which pass such a test. Is

[1] Even if the answer were in the negative—if there were no narrowly "economic" case for allocation by government—one could not rule out preference for modes of organization other than laissez-faire markets on quite different grounds. A fastidious humanitarian, for instance, might argue that to organize society so as to take advantage of man's instinct for material self-aggrandizement is bound to demean the human spirit and hence is immoral, no matter how much more efficient such organization may be in catering to "standard of living" values. On the other hand, a European-type liberal may hold that a variety of political and social non-output values relating to the configuration of power, opportunity, etc., are so much better served by some form of even grossly inefficient market institutions than by possible alternative modes of more efficient organization as to warrant choice of the former. But these are different matters; here my concern is with a price-market system not as an end, nor even as a means to noneconomic political and ethical ends, but simply as an organizational device for catering to consumers' wants. In particular, I am not concerned with the right "freely" to choose in markets. (See, however, Chapter 8.)

this so with regard to all activities? What is there of truth and error in the notion of market efficiency?[2]

The full answer, as it has emerged during the course of a century and a half of polemics and careful analysis, is unavoidably technical, being based on perhaps the most subtle insights of modern economic theory.[3] Yet its essence is simple enough. Imagine a world (1) where each individual's market choices reflect a subjective *preference ordering* which permits him to register preference or indifference as between any two bundles of goods and services independently of any other person's choices; (2) where the input-output decisions of each producer—his decisions about how much labor and raw material to buy, what machines to use, how much of what to produce, etc.—reflect a single-minded urge to maximize profit, subject only to the state of the production arts and market prices; and (3) where there exist very many independent buyers and sellers in every market, and hence a state of perfect competition. It can be shown that in such a world the particular allocation and distribution of scarce resources brought about by the separate decisions of millions of profit-maximizing producers and by the consumption and leisure-work decisions of

[2] In the notion, to take a significant recent formulation, that "when it comes to the advancing and expanding of our economy, that is by and large the business of Americans; the federal government can help, but . . . *our federal money will never be spent so intelligently and in so useful a fashion for the economy as will the expenditures that would be made by the private citizen, the taxpayer, if he hadn't had so much of it funneled off into the Federal Government.*" (President Eisenhower, January 14, 1959, cited in Transcript of News Conference, *New York Times,* January 15, 1959, p. 18; my italics.)

[3] And on a line of thought that goes back to Adam Smith, Ricardo, Mill, Walras, and Marshall. Important modern contributions have been made by Vilfredo Pareto, Enrico Barone, Knut Wicksell, and Professor A. C. Pigou, all writing just before World War I, and more recently by Abram Bergson, A. P. Lerner, and Paul Samuelson, and by H. Hotelling, J. R. Hicks, and Oscar Lange. For a detailed technical exposition, see my "The Simple Analytics of Welfare Maximization," *American Economic Review,* March 1957, pp. 22-59.

millions of consumers, all facing competitively determined prices in every market, will tend to be *efficient*. In what sense? In the very special sense that there will remain no possible reallocations, no shifts in inputs, outputs, and in distribution *such as would make some one or more individuals better off in terms of their own preferences without making some other individuals worse off in terms of theirs.*

It is easiest to think this through in terms of a simple parable. There exist two people, Crusoe and Friday; two kinds of producible goods, food and clothing; and two scarce inputs, labor and land, each useful in the production of both goods. Crusoe has exact knowledge of the various combinations of labor and land with which it is technically feasible to produce any specified amounts of food and of clothing (the economist's "production functions"). Moreover, both he and Friday have specified their own subjective preference orderings (one ordering for each) as among alternative bundles of food and clothing. Assume that these orderings are sensitive to own-consumption only, that Crusoe and Friday are each oblivious to the other's consumption.[4]

The problem of allocation, in this Crusoe and Friday world, is to fix ten numbers: the number of labor-hours to be used in food production (1); labor-hours to be used in clothing production (2); acres of land to be devoted to food (3) and to clothing (4); the total output of food (5) and of clothing (6); and the distribution of food and clothing between Friday and Crusoe (7-10). Clearly, there exists an infinite number of

[4] For the sake of simplicity, we assume that the total supply of each input is fixed—Crusoe and Friday both work ten hours a day; that neither cares about how he spends his ten hours; that every acre of land is like every other; and that an hour of Friday's labor is perfectly substitutable in both activities for an hour of Crusoe's. (We could perfectly well drop any of these assumptions, e.g., introduce any number of inputs and outputs, leisure-work choices, etc. Nonmathematical exposition would be very cumbersome, but nothing that matters for the argument would change.)

feasible solutions—allocations that are consistent with the technical input requirements of producing food and clothing and which do not require more labor and land than are available. However, *most* feasible solutions are inefficient, i.e., leave unexploited possible reallocations which would make both Friday and Crusoe better off. If, for instance, to take an extreme case, all land were allocated to food and all labor to clothing or vice versa, they would certainly end up with less both of food and of clothing than would be feasible. Or even if production were efficient, if the outputs were distributed so as to leave Friday with a surfeit of food but freezing, while Crusoe, with enough clothes for the North Pole, starved, there would be scope for redistribution which would please both. (In a situation where allocation *is* efficient, any redistribution of food and clothing which leaves Crusoe with a bundle he prefers to the one he started with will, *by the definition of efficiency,* leave Friday with a bundle which he judges inferior to his original allotment; and any reallocation of land and labor which yields more clothing will cause the output of food to fall. Production efficiency is implied by, but does not imply, efficiency all-around.)

Crusoe's problem—assume that he is a perfectionist—is not just to avoid inefficient allocations but to find the full *set* of efficient solutions on which it is impossible to improve (i.e., the "menu" of all possible combinations which leave no scope for benefiting the one without hurting the other). To do so in a world of only ten variables is not too difficult. With some knowledge of the calculus and modern algebra, and some luck with the mathematical characteristics of the technical production relations between inputs and outputs and the two preference orderings, solving the problem by centralized calculation is perfectly feasible. Moreover, once Crusoe and Friday have managed to decide which one of the many efficient solutions is to be chosen—i.e., have managed to "solve" the political-ethical problem of interpersonal distribution, perhaps by Crusoe's benevolent but dictatorial order—the problem of administration and enforcement is trivial (unless, of course, Friday feels enough put-upon to disobey).

What if we add more people, goods, and kinds of scarce inputs? As long as the data (production functions and preference orderings) are fully specified and still "well behaved," mathematical *computation,* while increasingly burdensome even with giant computers, would not become impossible in concept; feasibility would depend on the size and speed of the computing machinery. But the problem of administration and enforcement is not so easily fobbed off, even in "concept"; Crusoe cannot just be *assumed* able to police a million Fridays. Explicit attention must be given to organization, to incentives and sanctions. Moreover, if preference orderings are not recorded on punch cards in a Bureau of Tastes and if there exists no up-to-date catalogue of production functions for everything from hairpins to high-fidelity amplifiers, the entire problem, the joint problem of computation and administration, changes character. There is evident need for an organizational scheme which can do without a central catalogue of tastes and techniques, and can generate and enforce efficient allocation with a much reduced agenda of central computation.

This is where markets come in. A competitive price-market system based on private property is just such an organizational device. By decentralizing decisions to the individual consumer who need only be aware of market prices to act so as to maximize his satisfaction in terms of his own personal preferences, and to the individual producer who can be blissfully ignorant of all but prices and his own production function, a competitive market system secures just those economies of information handling without which, in the absence of a central catalogue, we would be badly stuck. At the same time it has built in, as it were, a scheme of incentives and sanctions in the form of profits and losses which will, if only producers will respond to the lure of money, render the maximizing rules and the price signals self-enforcing; a producer who is not responsive to prices and fails to maximize will lose his shirt and be driven out of business. Moreover, and this is the crucial point, given the assumptions made above about the independence of preferences and the feasibility of perfect competition, these economies of information handling and enforcement are "costless"—markets will yield efficient solutions. Each producer, concerned only with his own profit, and each consumer, bent on getting the most out of what he has, will do precisely what is needed to exhaust all mutually advantageous reallocations. Just this, in fact, is the sum and substance of Adam Smith's famed theorem of the "invisible hand."[5]

It would not be appropriate here—sadly, because it is a thing of beauty—to set out in detail the analytical content of the theorem. Its kernel lies in the remarkable fact that the mathematics of solving the problem of efficiency makes use of a set of auxiliary variables ("unknowns") *which turn out to have all the earmarks of prices, wage rates, interest rates, and rents*. This in the double sense that (1) the computational procedure involved in finding an efficient combination of inputs, outputs, and distribution happens to yield, as a byproduct, numerical magnitudes for these auxiliary variables which correspond precisely to the prices on which competitive markets would settle to cause supply to match demand in every market; and (2) that profit- and preference-maximizing decisions by millions of producers and consumers, all responding to these price numbers, would yield just that pattern of inputs, outputs, and distribution which the mathematical solution of

[5] In precise technical language, the theorem asserts that the equilibrium conditions which characterize a system of perfectly competitive markets will, given our assumptions, exactly correspond to the conditions implied by the solution of the mathematical maximizing problem which defines efficiency.

the efficiency problem calls for. What this implies is that the rules followed, e.g., by competing producers bent on maximizing their own profits, are precisely the rules they must follow if allocation is to be efficient. *Example:* a profit-eager producer facing competitively determined prices will increase his output up to where the increase in total cost due to the last unit, i.e., *marginal* cost, just equals the increase in revenue he can get by selling the last unit, i.e., price. But marginal-cost-equal-to-price can be shown to be just the rule producers *must* follow if their input-output decisions are to lead to efficient allocation.

What Role for Government Spending?

If a price-market "game" is a flawlessly efficient computing device with a more or less workable institutional counterpart, what sense is there in bypassing markets? It would be beside the point to cite paternalistic values, such as might require coercion to frustrate my taste, or yours, for morphine (even if indulged in perfect privacy). Nor would it be fair, given the level of abstraction of the previous argument, to stake the case on such "real life" imperfections of price-market institutions as may be due to, say, inertia on the part of producers. The question we must ask, rather, is whether there is not a case for government spending even in a world of single-minded and error-free profit- and preference-maximizing calculation, where consumers' tastes are really all that count.

Transfer Expenditure[6]

Paradoxically, the justification for pure transfer expenditure is suggested by the very case for market allocation. The use of markets was "justified" above in terms of their efficiency in catering to consumers' tastes. But which consumer's tastes?

[6] Recall that transfer expenditure redistributes income but does not constitute a claim on resources (cf. pp. 9-10).

How much weight is to be given to Crusoe's as against Friday's? How, to take a less rustic context, are dollar votes to be distributed among people? The ethical postulate that we should do as well as possible by consumers' tastes provides no answer. It is neutral as among the *infinite* number of efficient solutions, which range from all food and all clothing going to Crusoe to where everything goes to Friday.[7]

Laissez-faire markets, in contrast, are anything but neutral. With given initial ownership of the "means of production" (in a Crusoe world, labor and land), markets will yield a particular configuration of inputs and outputs and also of *distribution among people*. Under "ideal" circumstances, moreover, this will be an efficient configuration. But will it be the "best" of the efficient combinations or the "worst," or the hundredth best? There exist no considerations of economic *efficiency* which would permit us to say. Choice among efficient combinations involves ultimate ethical values (call them "equity values"), and it would be sheer accident if the particular efficient configuration generated by markets turned out to rate higher in terms of my ethical valuations, or yours, or Thomas Jefferson's, or that of a politically engineered "consensus," than all other efficient, and even many inefficient, solutions.[8]

But all is not lost. It is evidently not true that to secure the efficiency vouchsafed by competitive markets we must accept

[7] The fact that such extremely unequal allocations may be inefficient because Friday needs food or clothes to work gives rise to no difficulty. Subsistence needs and incentive effects can easily be taken account of in deciding on the efficient set of allocations.

[8] It is true, given an *in*efficient outcome, that there will exist (some) efficient outcomes that would be better in the sense of making some (or all) people better off and no one worse off. But there may well be many efficient outcomes that would be much worse in terms of any particular ethic. Someone with egalitarian predilections, for instance, may well prefer an *in*efficient solution which yields a fairly balanced distribution of income to an efficient solution (more of *both* food and clothing) which, however, leaves very much to Crusoe and very little to Friday.

the distribution of income generated by such markets. It is possible to break the link between ownership and "final" income distribution by means of tax-financed interpersonal "transfers" and to do so without exempting any allocations from a private market test.[9] In fact, this is precisely what is done. Government spending on old-age assistance, on veterans' cash bonuses, and the like does not cause resources to bypass markets; it simply redistributes command over resources among people. The final spending for goods and services is by private individuals bidding in markets, guided by their personal preferences.[10]

Exhaustive Expenditure and Subsidies

The case for or against pure transfer expenditure cannot be resolved, it appears, by invoking the doctrine of consumer sovereignty; explicit attention must be given to the ethics and politics of income distribution. But what about government

[9] For discussion of the point that it is not really costless to do so—that taxes and transfers give rise to inefficiency, see p. 104.

[10] It is a different matter that some hold any such redistribution wrong on *ethical* grounds, as violating the "natural right" of everyone to his property, or to what he earns, or to what he is "worth" on the market. To ascribe ethical significance to the particular distribution of income effected by markets is to introduce a value judgment over and above the value of efficiently catering to consumers' tastes.

Incidentally, the choice between *present* consumption, on the one hand, and saving for investment for future consumption, on the other, involves precisely the same sort of ethical issues of interpersonal distribution as the question of current income distribution. There exists no criterion of efficiency which would permit us to fix the balance between consumption and investment for the community as a whole; again, we need interpersonal ("intergenerational") ethics. Once the balance is fixed for society as a whole, and granted only the ethical postulate that I am to be responsible for my *own* future, efficiency implies that I be allowed to make my current saving-consumption decisions as I see fit. It remains the task of tax and interest policy to secure consistency between the personal decisions of individuals and the political-ethical "decision" of the community.

purchases of goods and services and subsidies? Is there any justification, in terms of the principle of efficiently catering to consumers' tastes, for bypassing a market test and allocating some resources via political procedures?[11]

The answer hangs on the validity of the assumptions about preferences and conditions of production which are necessary for the "invisible hand" theorem to hold. In the above discussion of market efficiency, these assumptions, while repeatedly mentioned, were treated rather lightly. Yet it is the failure of the assumptions even approximately to match the facts of the real world that constitutes the core of the strictly "economic" case for public spending.[12]

The most serious philosophical difficulties concern the assumption—and it is an assumption of fact—that individuals' tastes (i.e., preference orderings) are insensitive to other people's consumption (or preference orderings). This rules out all Veblenesque "keeping up with . . ." effects, all interactions based on fashion or repugnance. It leaves out of account the outrage perpetrated on X's temperance sensibilities by Y's quiet and solitary consumption of Scotch; the influence on X's job satisfaction of his *relative* power, status, etc. Further, it ignores

[11] Or, in the case of subsidies, of modifying the effect of the market test?

[12] That such an "economic" case is too narrow a foundation for even an "economic" theory of government is almost too obvious to warrant comment. Indeed, some may feel that to explore what justification there may be for government spending in terms of the ethical postulates of Manchester liberalism is a foolish waste of time, especially since it requires that we take a rather abstract view of markets. Yet quite apart from the analytical insight the exercise may offer, it is not clear to me that the "Manchester view" either is, or indeed that it ought to be, so dead as to warrant the charge of irrelevance. Its significance cannot be measured by the number of people who cling to its substance. By providing the rhetoric and the implicit ground rules which govern public disputation on economic matters, it holds us captive even while we think we know better. In America, at least, the clichés of Ricardian economics, if not its substance, still dominate debate. (It would be better were it more the other way round.)

all vicarious pleasure or displeasure I may take in other people's enjoyment of *their* consumption. (The fact that there are no rules against charity helps some but not enough.) Yet to salvage the "invisible hand" one must either assume that these taste interactions are empirically insignificant or adopt the distinctly paternalistic view that, significant or not, they are not to count. The good Manchester liberal may feel averse to forcing strawberries and cream down reluctant throats, but imposition of the virtue of tolerance—by the use of an organizational scheme which frustrates one's sovereign taste for intolerance—is apparently a different matter. (And, of course, it *is* a different matter. Once we admit that the value of "consumer sovereignty" is no more *absolute* than other values—that it is, in fact, inconsistent with other values likely to be important to the same people to whom liberal individualism is important—then the hard truth that compromise with lesser evil is unavoidable if gross evil is to be avoided, instead of posing a hopeless dilemma, becomes the very stuff on which to exercise one's political and ethical faculties.)

With direct interaction of preferences, decentralization of allocation decisions via flawlessly competitive markets can no longer be assumed costless; private decisions will waste opportunities for making some people better off without hurting others. But what if the problem did not exist—if people's tastes really were sensitive only to own-consumption (and own-labor)? Then would markets do? Would all reallocations which make someone better off without hurting anyone else turn out to be commercially profitable for some producer or trader? Unfortunately (from the point of view of anyone for whom the organizational simplicity and decentralizing power of the price system has a strong appeal), the truth is less than kind. If we care about consumers' preferences, we must cope with two related technical characteristics of the real world which cause decentralized market calculation to be grossly inefficient

—economies of scale in production, and the prevalence of what the economist calls "public goods."

Where the "Invisible Hand" Fails (1)

Competition requires that there be "very many" producers in every market. If economies of large-scale production confer a cost advantage on firms that are large relative to the total market, a few technically efficient producers will saturate the market, and competition, in the technical sense, will break down. Each producer will be large enough for his *own* output decisions to have an appreciable effect on price. This in turn will cause the profit-minded producer to fix his output at a level where marginal cost is less than price, i.e., at a level lower than is required for efficient allocation. Output will fall short of where the extra cost to society is just covered by extra benefit as measured by price.[13]

Nor can antitrust action, no matter how ideally designed, correct the situation. While useful in controlling or eliminating concentration of market power which is based on other than

[13] The technical reason is simple enough. While, for *efficient* allocation, output should be increased up to where the extra cost of the last unit just equals the *price* people are willing to pay, the producer is interested in the balance between extra cost and extra (i.e., *marginal*) revenue. In a competitive market where, to take an example, an increase in a single farmer's output will not appreciably reduce the price of wheat, the extra revenue that accrues to the farmer if he sells an extra bushel is just equal to the price. But where a single producer is large enough relative to the market to take account of the effect on price of changes in his *own* output, his marginal revenue will no longer equal price. Marginal revenue on, say, the 101st unit of output will equal, rather, the price on the 101st *less* the reduction in revenue (i.e., the sales value) on the first 100 units due to the drop in market price which is caused by throwing the 101st unit on the market. Hence at the level of output at which the producer's total profit is at a maximum, i.e., where the extra revenue due to the last unit is just equal to the extra cost, such extra (marginal) cost will be less than price. People would be willing to pay more for an additional unit of output than the extra cost involved in producing it.

technical or administrative economies of large-scale production (e.g., concentration based on financial advantages of size due to imperfections in capital markets), trying to maintain many small units if there are true resource economies to be had by large-scale production is obviously a self-defeating procedure.[14]

Price regulation of the right sort, as approximated by the best public utility commissions, is more akin to what is needed. A publicly administered price, if it allows for positive profit, will induce as-if competitive behavior. For maximum profit, output will be increased up to where marginal cost is just covered by the centrally fixed price. But even this fails to get at the heart of the matter. It fails, notably, to take account of the curious fact that the price-output combination required for efficient allocation may well imply negative profits, i.e., continuing losses.

The key to this paradox lies in the meaning of "economies of scale." The existence of scale economies at a given level of output means no more nor less than that a small increase in output from that level will cause unit cost (cost per unit: total cost divided by output) to fall. It happens, moreover, that at such a point of declining *unit* cost, marginal cost: the increment in total cost due to an extra unit of output, is necessarily less than unit cost.[15] Yet it is generally still true that, if allocation is to be efficient, output must be increased up to where

[14] This is not to gainsay that antitrust measures can reduce some of the undesirable effects of concentration. But their proper role is not to try to maintain the world as it would be if perfect competition were feasible. Rather, it is to serve as one of a variety of complementary instruments of social control appropriate to a world where perfect competition is not feasible.

[15] In fact, it is the difference between *marginal* cost and *unit* cost that causes unit cost to fall as output is increased. If unit cost were $1.00 and marginal cost $1.00, why should unit cost fall? The increase in total cost due to an extra unit of output would be $1.00 and unit cost, i.e., total cost divided by output, would remain $1.00. But if unit cost at an output of 20 units is $1.00, while the increase in total cost

marginal cost is just covered by price. But if price is to equal marginal cost where marginal cost is less than unit cost, price must be less than unit cost. Evidently efficiency requires that producers operating in a range of decreasing cost operate at a loss. Evidently, also, no profit-seeking producer will long do so.[16]

Consider, for example, the "production" of bridge crossings. Assume, to take an extreme instance, that once the bridge in question is built, all wear and tear is a function of time rather than use, i.e., that there are no additional costs associated with extra crossings. (The bridge is never so full as to give rise to crowding.) The marginal cost to society, in terms of scarce resources, of an additional crossing is zero. It follows—the proposition is mathematically demonstrable, as well as, in this case, intuitively obvious—that the efficient ration price for a crossing is precisely zero. A positive price such as would discourage even a single crossing would cause allocation to be inefficient; there would remain unexploited a costless crossing which could make someone better off without hurting anyone else. Yet it is equally evident that charging a price of zero for crossings will hardly raise sufficient revenue to cover the cost of building the bridge.

It is tempting to argue that if this is the case, if the bridge cannot pay for itself, then it should not be built. But this is not even plausible. It implies that no facility with a large fixed (initial) cost and relatively low *variable* cost (and therefore

---

due to the 21st unit is only \$.50, the unit cost of 21 units would be $\frac{20 \times \$1 + 1 \times \$.50}{21} = \frac{\$20.50}{21}$, or less than \$1.00.

[16] Where market imperfections are pervasive, there are also other difficulties with the rule that output be increased to where marginal cost equals price. If one is trying to get nine drunks who are tied to each other to walk in a straight line, it may not help to sober up one of them.

low marginal cost) should ever be built. (It is just such high fixed-cost and low variable-cost facilities that are characterized by unit costs which decline with output; it is simply a matter of spreading the "fixed" overhead.) Not only bridges but also roads, railroads, airfields, dams, ports, would all be ruled out as uneconomic. But of course the proposition is indefensible. It is easy to prove that where technology gives rise to economies of scale at the relevant levels of output, profitability at a competitive price is not a necessary condition of efficiency. The test of profit breaks down.[17]

Nor, by the way, is monopoly a satisfactory way out. It is true that in many cases where competition is unworkable—where one or a few firms are bound by reason of scale efficiency to saturate the market—monopolists or a few large oligopolists, so-called, could all make a profit. It may well be, for instance, that there is a positive price at which the operation of our bridge would be profitable, i.e., would more than cover cost. It may even be that such private monopolistic operation is the best of the administratively and politically feasible organizational devices for getting the bridge built and operated. But the fact remains that any such noncompetitive rationing of crossings by a price calculated to maximize net revenue results in less-than-efficient allocation. Bridge crossings would be restricted below the number which would just equate the cost of

[17] To a sophisticated businessman used to running a decentralized multi-division firm all this would not come as too much of a surprise. Not every process in a well-run firm should be expected to cover its cost in terms of the right set of internal accounting prices. *Total* profit is the deciding criterion, and it may be worth while for a firm to build a private bridge between its two installations on opposite sides of a river yet charge a zero accounting price for its use by the various decentralized manufacturing and administrative divisions. (Zero would certainly be the right price if a positive accounting price discouraged the use of the bridge while extra use involved no extra cost.) The bridge considered as a separate activity would make accounting losses, yet total company profits would be increased.

the last crossing to offer-price. In our example, where marginal cost is zero, some socially *costless* crossings would be discouraged. It would be possible to increase the output of crossings without decreasing the output of anything else.[18]

Monopoly, moreover, may not even be a second-best answer, not even with appropriate "discipline" imposed by public agencies staffed by administrators straight out of Plato. It is entirely possible wherever economies of scale are substantial that there is no price which would cover the cost of a facility which nevertheless is required for efficient allocation. It is an old but still intriguing proposition of economics that an activity may be necessary for efficiency though even monopoly operation would fail to cover its cost. The only true test is provided by a perfectly "discriminating" monopolist, so called, who manages for every single crossing to squeeze out of every single customer the maximum toll that the individual is prepared to pay to be permitted that one crossing. The resources that go into a bridge can be shown to be misallocated only if such a perfectly discriminating monopolist, who confronts every user at every crossing with a lump-sum, take-it-or-leave-it offer which reflects a perfect assessment of the customer's desire for that crossing, should fail to cover the cost of the bridge.[19]

The moral of all this is plain. As regards activities characterized by economies of large-scale production (at levels of output which are relevant in terms of the volume of demand), a price-market system, while it may still serve to raise revenue to cover cost, will no longer be simultaneously efficient in rationing

[18] Note that the effect on allocation is quite distinct from what usually worries people about monopoly—its effect on income distribution.

[19] Put differently, there exist many situations where no single "admission" price would raise sufficient revenue to cover the cost of an establishment, e.g., of a repertory theater company where, however, lump-sum contributions based on an "all plays free or no theater" choice, would, if only people could be made honestly to own up to their preferences, amply cover cost. (The qualification about "owning up" has to do with the problem of "publicness" discussed in the next section.)

output. Alternatively, the price which will efficiently ration output will fail to raise sufficient revenue to avoid loss. Monopolistic operation (at price greater than marginal cost) may or may not succeed in covering cost; where so, however, there will be inefficient curtailment of output. And where not, subsidy may be unavoidable if there is to be any output whatever.

This is the sum and substance of the *qualitative* case, in terms of efficiency, against exclusive reliance on the test of profit as concerns such things as railroads, airlines, roads, public parks, public libraries, river-valley development, and perhaps even the postal services. All these activities are characterized by decreasing unit cost at the relevant levels of output. Competition, in the economist's sense, is not feasible. In some cases monopolistic operation may yield a "full-cost" price, but, since by the very nature of the situation a price which covers unit cost will exceed marginal cost, the result is misallocation. In other cases, there exists no full-cost price, i.e., no price which will yield enough revenue to cover cost, and it is impossible to get any output without subsidy (barring, perhaps, only a very sophisticated structure of differential prices). If we take seriously the case for efficiently catering to consumers' preferences, unadulterated markets will not do.[20]

Where the "Invisible Hand" Fails (2)

Where marginal cost is positive but less than unit cost, efficient allocation (in an ideal world) requires that output be

[20] It does not follow, of course, that we should give up on market mediation in *all* or even most sectors of the economy where decreasing-cost activities predominate. Inefficient markets may often do much better than any feasible alternative mode of organization. (To cite only one reason, subsidies require taxes, which in turn give rise to inefficiency.) The point is only that we cannot count on market decisions to lead to even approximately efficient allocation when it comes to strongly decreasing-cost activities; that to allocate resources to such activities according to their commercial profitability may be exceedingly costly. (For comment on the problem of choosing among various inefficient "solutions," see pp. 108-112.)

rationed by a price equal to marginal cost and that the resulting losses be subsidized. This is typically the situation in so-called public utilities. Additional use entails some additional cost, but the initial fixed cost of the facility, whether it be a port, a dam, a thermal station, or a railroad line, is so high relative to costs which vary with the rate at which the facility is used that unit cost declines with output, and equality of price and marginal cost implies operating in the red.

There are activities, however, where the additional cost of extra use is literally zero. The economist labels the output of such activities "public." A good or service is defined as public if X's consumption of it leads to no subtraction from what is left over for consumption by Y and Z. Radio programs, the services rendered by the beacon atop the Statue of Liberty, the protection provided by the Strategic Air Command are some examples. The additional resource costs of an extra TV viewer, of an extra listener at an uncrowded open air concert, of an additional child watching a fireworks display, of a newly naturalized citizen benefiting from the deterrent-potential of the "Nautilus," of the "Queen Mary" as well as the "Liberté" taking directional guidance from a lighthouse beacon—all are zero. Hence, for efficient allocation, price too must be zero. Pay television may be judged preferable to having to listen to toothpaste advertisements every fifteen minutes, but if it involves charging anyone a positive price for doing something that does not cost anyone else a penny, i.e., for tuning-in, it leads to inefficient allocation (though perhaps less so than does the advertising).[21]

[21] Again, the proposition that price must be zero is not a dictum based on intuition but a theorem subject to formal proof. And again, it is subject to the qualification that it *may* in some instances be less inefficient to use the price system to raise the revenue required to cover the cost of a facility than to use taxes (even though this implies charging a positive price that will cause misallocation). But commercial profitability is a very poor indicator of whether a facility whose ser-

Examples of *pure* public goods are few. Most things, even battleships and certainly open-air concerts and schools (though *not* knowledge), have an "if-more-for-you-then-less-for-me" quality. But this is of little comfort. If a commodity or a service has even a trace of "publicness," be it only in the form of by-product effects which impinge inseparably on many people, then profit- and preference-seeking market calculation will not efficiently mediate its production and distribution. Hence the obvious fact that such things as urban renewal, hospital facilities, education, research, street lighting, vaccination programs, parks, police protection, and the like yield benefits of a "more-for-you-means-no-less-for-me" sort guarantees that market decisions with regard to these activities will fail to do justice to consumers' tastes.

It is sometimes alleged, mistakenly, that the nub of the difficulty lies in the "inability" of a producer of a public good physically to exclude users or to control the rationing of his produce among them, i.e., with "divorce of scarcity from effective ownership." The implication is that if only it weren't impossible, clumsy, costly, or illegal to "keep book" on who produces and who gets what and to enforce payment, all would be well. It is evident that for pure public goods this is not so. It is entirely *feasible* to "own" a bridge, and perhaps profitably to ration crossings; indeed, a private owner would do so. But, as was emphasized above, such profitable rationing, such "compensation" for services rendered, would inefficiently misallocate the output of bridge crossings. If in terms of alternative opportunities the extra cost of an additional crossing is zero, the

---

vices are "public" in the technical sense is worth having to start off with. (If the assertion that the theorem about zero price is subject to proof seems puzzling, recall that allocation was defined as efficient if the configuration of inputs, outputs, and distribution corresponds exactly to the solution of a mathematical maximum problem with given constraints.)

only price consistent with efficiency is, once again, zero. Ditto for, say, TV programs or that most valuable of assets, new knowledge.[22]

In a sense, as use of the bridge as an example has already implied, a "public good" situation is simply a polar instance of decreasing costs. Yet it leads more directly to the core of the case for tax-financed government spending than does the ordinary decreasing-cost model. The latter tends to draw one's attention to the problem of motivating producers to produce something the ration price of which, to be efficient, must be less than unit cost. This certainly requires subsidies, but why coercive, mandatory taxation? Why cannot everybody be counted on to contribute according to his anticipation of subjective, own-taste-determined benefit? Moreover, would not the sum raised by such voluntary contributions accurately reflect people's tastes for, say, a mosquito-control program, and hence provide us with just the measure of consumer benefit we need to match against the cost?

Unfortunately, the very condition which gives rise to the

[22] It would not be impossible, after all, by strengthening patent and copyright protection, to increase substantially the power of the originator to appropriate, i.e., to cash in on, the benefits of a valuable idea. (TV shows, in turn, and also radar-equipped lighthouses, could be protected from free-riders by means of electronic "scramblers.") But it is the essence of public goods that reward by ration price would be inefficient. To be efficient in rationing scarcities the price system must fail in its rewards; and if it is used to reward, it will reward the wrong things.

There are, of course, situations where exclusion is *the* binding consideration, where certain "goods" or "bads" with determinate and "profitable" efficiency prices are not (easily) appropriated. The cost to a producer of training a laborer is a case in point. The social benefit accrues over the working lifetime of the trainee; the private benefit to the producer accrues until the man quits to go to work for a competitor. The "fault" lies in the Emancipation Proclamation and in such imperfections of the capital market as make it difficult for the trainee to borrow in order to invest in himself at rates appropriate to a reasonable estimate of risk and expected return.

need for a subsidy will cause a system of voluntary contributions to misrepresent people's tastes for public goods. Sharing of *private* goods in proportion to voluntary "contributions"—which is precisely what happens where goods are rationed by price in competitive markets—is efficient because a "sensible" economic man's "contributions," his dollar purchases, accurately reflect his preference ordering. He contributes to the financing of apple production, that is, he buys apples, until the last nickel spent on apples yields just enough apples to compensate him for forgoing five cents' worth of nuts and pipe cleaners. He so "reveals" his tastes, however, only because to get apples he must pay for them, because apples will be available to him for consumption in proportion to what he spends. If apples were like firework displays, or mosquito-control programs, or open-air concerts on the neighbor's lawn, in other words, if his consumption of apples were a function not of how many he paid for but of their *total* supply, then his dollar contribution or purchase would hardly reflect his true tastes. Especially if he is one of many, he would be tempted to "understate" his desire for such "apples," i.e., for public goods, in the hope that other people would shoulder a higher share of the cost without his forgoing any of the benefit. Or conceivably, if he is one of a few and if the total cost of the facility relative to his pocketbook is small, he might underestimate others' eagerness and "overpay," ending up, and unnecessarily so, with more of public and less of private goods than he would like. But whether he underpays or overpays—and as regards costly activities (e.g., national defense) the latter is unlikely—the poker-like bluffing and dissimulation intrinsic to the problem of sharing the cost of public goods will cause not only simple allocation by price but also more elaborate systems of financing by voluntary contribution to be grossly unreliable in fixing the balance between public and private goods. It would always be possible, by changing the balance, to do what would never be feasible in a frictionless free-market world of pure private goods—make everyone better off.

We need not pursue the fine detail.[23] The point is clear enough—public good and decreasing cost phenomena cause private market decisions to go wrong. Market prices will fail to approximate true scarcity values in terms of wants; they will be loaded with misinformation, and producers' profit calculations will leave out of account much of the private benefit associated with public goods. The "invisible hand" will fumble: people's decentralized market choices will not efficiently cater to their tastes. If tastes matter, the community must take communal responsibility for the balance between private and public goods. The proposition that government has a significant allocating function turns out to be a corollary of the doctrine of consumer sovereignty.[24, 25]

[23] Anyone interested should consult Paul Samuelson's originating development of the theory of public goods in the *Review of Economics and Statistics* (November 1954, 1955, and 1958).

[24] The fact that people's market choices do badly by their *own* tastes is a paradox only in a trivial sense. If one adopts the useful fiction of "rationality"—as I have done throughout—a man will by definition so choose as to do the best by his own tastes, *given the environment* (i.e., prices). But he will do so whether the ratio of the price of Cadillacs to the price of lollypops is thirty thousand to one or one to thirty thousand. If the latter price ratio prevailed he would still do the best he could, but since the real opportunity cost of Cadillacs is in fact much greater than that of lollypops, market choices would hardly do well by tastes. If it is the right to choose that matters, any set of prices invented by an O.P.A. man gone berserk would do as well as any other.

[25] For a technical discussion of the various modes and causes of market failure, see my "The Anatomy of Market Failure," *Quarterly Journal of Economics*, August 1958, pp. 351-379.

7 | THE ALLOCATION OF SCARCE RESOURCES (3)

Inefficient Markets versus Inefficient Government

I HAVE explored the case against markets in terms of the ethical postulate of consumer sovereignty and within the framework of price theory not because I think that this "case" either exhausts the reasons for public spending or necessarily justifies such spending—nor because it provides positive answers to the immensely difficult problems of allocation and social organization posed by the existence of public goods. The fact is that it tells us little about what mix of organizational devices will keep us from going astray. If the case is worth making, it is in order to do away with simple-minded answers that are wrong, and not because it provides any simple answers that are right.

Even on these modest terms, however, much of the above would be beside the point if publicly financed activities did not exhibit a strong public quality, or if it were reasonable to think that as a general rule, and even as regards strongly public activities, allocation by government spending is likely to be more inefficient than inefficient markets. It happens, however, that fact and reason suggest otherwise.

Is Public Money Spent on Public Goods?

As to the first issue, the gross facts suggest that the bulk of federal as well as state and local purchases in 1957, for instance, were for services with a strong decreasing-cost/public-good quality. *Without implying anything whatever about the detailed project complexion of the various major programs, or about the merits of the organizational devices being used, or, most emphatically, about the appropriate quantitative scale of such programs,* it is evident that it cannot simply be assumed that market mediation would have done better by people's wants than did public allocation as regards national defense; general government; international affairs and finance; public health and sanitation; education; police, fire-protection, and prisons; regulation of commerce and finance; highway, water, and air transportation; transit, electricity, water, gas, and postal services; and conservation, development, and recreational use of natural resources. In 1957 these categories accounted for 96.8 per cent of public purchases of goods and services (Table 6).

About the other 3.2 per cent ($2.81 billion) of G, horseback judgment is more difficult even in gross qualitative terms, especially since most of the money was used to support programs the primary purpose of which is to provide income compensation to particular groups of people (i.e., to redistribute income). Expenditure on veterans' hospitals and medical care ($813 million, all federal) and on veterans' education and training ($9 million) is clearly of this sort, yet it can perhaps be defended in terms of the public quality of the services rendered. Equivalent cash disbursements to veterans would not have resulted in equivalent allocations to hospital facilities even if veterans' own preferences had called for such allocations. The same is true of the $185 million (all but $9 million of it state-local) that was spent on housing and community redevelopment.[1] On the other hand, the $895 million of G-type expenditure on public assistance and relief and on old-age retirement benefits, etc. (most of it federal-financed state-local spending) is best defended—if it is to be defended—on grounds of income distribution. Preference for services in kind over outright cash grants cannot easily be justified except in paternalistic terms.[2]

This leaves unaccounted-for $261 million of (net) purchases of goods and services under the "agriculture" rubric and $3.14 billion of federal spending which the Commerce Department labels "subsidies less current surplus of government enterprises."[3] Of this last, $176 million went for highways and water- and air-transport, $9 million for housing and community redevelopment, and $545 million for the postal services —all activities which would fare badly if left to markets. The bulk of the money, however—$2.73 billion of subsidies and the $261 million of G—was accounted for by agriculture, with $2.48 billion going to stabilize farm prices and income.[4] For

[1] Housing expenditure yields output that is partially public because people care about the physical character of the neighborhood they and their children's schoolmates live in, and hence at least some of the benefit accrues inseparably to many people.

Some of the $299 million spent on "labor and manpower" (mostly federal-grant-financed state-local G) is also of this sort. It is used in part to cover the cost of administering unemployment compensation and employment service activities, to finance the Bureau of Apprenticeship and Training, etc.

[2] It does not follow, however, that it cannot be justified. Few people seriously believe that the world would be a better place if literally *all* paternalistic measures designed to protect people against themselves were scrapped.

[3] Plus some $352 million of miscellaneous administrative expenditure labeled as "other," most of it in two categories: veterans' services, and commerce and housing. Incidentally, the percentages are relative to G gross of the $422 million of government sales.

[4] Total subsidies exceeded $3.14 billion by the amount of profits earned by federal enterprises.

this, of all major programs, the public-good argument contains no defense. Income maintenance is the prime consideration, and it is a sad commentary on our politics that we have been unable to agree on a less devious and less wasteful means to achieve the desired end.[5, 6]

Markets versus Government

Agriculture aside, then, free markets would not do well by most of the major functions now served by government. It is frequently argued, however, that government does not do well either—that in general, and apart from defense and law enforcement, even less-than-efficient markets would be more efficient than allocation by government. The moral generally advanced is that any shift of resources from government to private use will cut inefficiency and hence be a good thing.

"Local" Inefficiency

Deferring comment for the moment about the serious and difficult problem of just what mix of institutional devices will do best where market choice does badly, what basis is there for the conventional view that governmental use of resources is prima facie less efficient than private market-directed alloca-

[5] Whether or not the end is justified is a matter of distributional ethics and not economic efficiency. (Ends and means do, of course, interact. The principal reason why we have not been able to work out a less wasteful stabilization program is that people disagree over the proper objectives of such a program. In particular, the major beneficiaries of the present program are quite aware that they cannot possibly gain political acceptance for an equally lucrative but more efficient arrangement such as would identify income redistribution from taxpayers in general to particular people who are now farmers as the objective of the program. And so far, the farm bloc has had enough political power to veto any change that would really hurt.)

[6] Gross G for agriculture was $805 million. Some of this, however, was probably for more or less public activities, e.g., for research, genuine conservation, electrification, etc.

tion? Garden-variety argumentation generally begins and ends with allegations of bureaucratic red tape, political shenanigans, and so on. The congenial premise is that large private bureaucracies are relatively immune to such "local" (i.e., operating) inefficiency, that in some sense private producers come closer to providing their output at minimum feasible cost than do public producers in providing theirs. Therefore, it is argued, less government means less waste.

Quite apart from the truth about "local" inefficiency—anecdotes are a poor substitute for careful study of comparative costs—the "therefore" rests on a double misapprehension. For one, it involves a confusion of government spending with government production. About half of what is paid for by government is produced by private, profit-guided producers and consists of goods and non-labor services which show up in government accounts under "cost of goods sold." (Most of the rest goes for the wages and salaries of government employees.) But more important, the argument involves a play on the word "efficiency." It does no good to demonstrate that private producers produce their output with less waste than does the government *its* output if markets cannot be counted on to induce private producers to provide the latter. If people want a public-health program, then to eliminate it because it is wastefully administered and because consumers would spend the money on wastelessly produced consumer goods is to follow the example of the man in Atlanta who wanted to go to New Orleans but decided to take the train to New York because it was faster. The problem of how to substitute for profit incentives in checking "local" inefficiency in public activities is not at all trivial, as anyone who has had dealings with the postal service will agree (though have you tried Railway Express?); but "solving" it by imposing an institutional regime which will assure relatively "efficient" production of the wrong things, i.e., which will guarantee gross inefficiency in terms of consumers' preferences, is to throw out not only the baby but the bathtub.[7]

The "Dead-weight" Costs of Taxes

A somewhat more sophisticated argument—more sophisticated in its premise if not in its conclusion—turns on the fact that the very process of transferring command over resources from income earners to government is "wasteful." It is wasteful (over and above any legitimate costs of administration) because any but an ideal and unfeasible system of lump-sum taxes will cause market prices to diverge from true scarcity values and hence cause people to miscalculate the real costs of their choices in terms of forgone alternatives. In particular, producers' cost-revenue calculations, based on market prices, will fail to reflect the true costs and benefits of alternative activities.

But to admit that tax-induced substitution effects give rise to waste, and specifically that they increase the real cost of tax-financed public goods and render even pure transfer payments burdensome by more than the cost of their administration, is to acknowledge only that the train to New York is faster. It no more warrants "going to New York" than does local inefficiency in public production. Sensible choice must be based, once again, on matching of opportunity cost (including cost that reflects waste) against benefit, generally not on an all-or-none basis but for marginal changes of scale.[8]

[7] It is true that by increasing the cost of public goods in terms of forgone private goods local inefficiency in the production of public goods will shift the efficient balance in favor of private goods. If the train to New Orleans is slow enough, even a sensible Atlantan might decide that he really *wants* to go to New York, or perhaps just to Augusta.

[8] "Only when we have lower tax rates will management and investors be free to make decisions on the basis of business factors and not for tax lures" is a typical formulation of the "inefficiency" argument for cutting tax rates. The hidden premise is that decisions on the basis

Dynamics

There is still a third argument often advanced in support of the rule that almost any shift from public to private spending will improve allocation; it turns on dynamical considerations of uncertainty and change. Indeed, ardent defenders of laissez-faire will have no doubt dismissed much of the above, with its assumption of unchanging tastes and techniques, as a blatant case of Hamlet-without-prince. Even the eclectic, who think of a market system, and rightly, as a powerful engine of technological advance and rising productivity, will have been concerned about the relevance of statical reasoning based on the fiction of a changeless world. But will they have been right?[9]

---

of "business factors" would be the *right* decisions, whereas we know that where decreasing-cost/public-good phenomena prevail, this is not so. The fallacy is identical to that which vitiates the local-inefficiency argument. (Quotation attributed, with no indication of context, to Professor Stanley Surrey of the Harvard Law School, by the November 1957 *Monthly Letter* of the First National City Bank of New York. The statement is taken from an article in *Collier's,* March 1956.)

Of course, one must not make the opposite mistake either. Tax-caused waste ought to be taken into account in determining the differential costs and benefits of any proposed public activity—the more so since such waste is likely to increase more than proportionately with the share of taxes in national income. On the other hand, tax reform is not illegal; a lot could be done to reduce tax waste without either reducing revenue or violating such norms about income distribution as are built into our politics.

[9] At the least, it is worth noting that people who stake their case for markets on the assertion that innovation renders statical reasoning irrelevant are their own worst enemies. The assertion cuts both ways. If it negates the public-good case for partially public allocation, it *ipso facto* destroys the core of the economic case for markets. If statical reasoning is irrelevant, what nonmystical basis is there for the claim that a price market system is an efficient instrument for catering to consumers? Luckily, the view that statical reasoning is irrelevant is indefensible. It is usually based on a naïve misunderstanding as to what theory, and indeed thought, is all about.

Take the least dramatic version of the dynamical claim for market superiority: that a market system will be quicker to correct mistakes, to fish or cut bait. Letting pass that this again has to do more with government production than government spending (and also the mixing of metaphor), aren't we back on the train to New York? True enough, where profitability is a necessary and sufficient test of efficiency, the fact that a private producer cannot long sustain losses by dipping into the public till is an advantage. But where profitability fails correctly to signal the true balance between cost and benefit, as in the case of activities which have a strong public quality, this is beside the point. Private producers will cut bait not only where there are no fish; they will pass up what may be the best fishing around. To equate the scuttling of activities which lose money with correction of mistakes is to miss what the public good problem is all about and to condone all sin by omission.

It is the more ironic that free markets are generally regarded as peculiarly immune to sin by omission. They are, it is held, a superior instrument for catering to consumers because they guarantee relentless exploitation of new techniques, new types of goods, of all ways for doing things cheaper and better. But which new techniques and which new goods? Sputniks and color television, nuclear power plants and wash-and-wear business suits, Salk vaccine and the "Nautilus," though all involve innovation, are hardly free: scarce capital and labor, scarce managers and physicists have to be shared among them. The crux of the issue, once again, is whether (expected) profitability is or is not an efficient indicator of (changing) wants and scarcities. Where it is, all is well. But where it is not, as where public goods are involved, the fact that market competition induces innovation is of small comfort. Profit-guided innovation will be misdirected; markets will fix on the wrong new things.

This is not to deny that innovation is important. An institutional setup which stimulates innovation, even a lot of misdirected innovation, *may* do much better than one which would work wonders in a context of unchanging tastes and techniques. But it surely does not follow that to do well by consumers we should give up on public goods and entrust all allocation choice, beyond defense and the enforcement of contracts, to markets. Indeed, it would not follow even if it were obvious that an economy with 25 per cent of final purchases by government is likely to be less innovative, in some sense, than an economy with government purchases at 10 per cent of GNP. But as a matter of fact, whatever the truth of the usual allegations about the effect of cost-plus arrangements on incentives, about the inflexibility of governmental customers, etc., the issue is not resolved by the relative innovativeness of, say, Chrysler in supplying its public as against its private customers. The really crucial questions concern the effects of public versus private spending on pure and applied research, on the tempo of pilot-plant development, and, most important, on the supply of intelligent people with advanced technical training. It is a bold man who would claim that we would be further ahead in the development and peaceful application of nuclear techniques, electronics, jet propulsion, agricultural husbandry, and disease prevention and control if during the past decade the government had not supported, directly and *indirectly,* a costly and commercially unsupportable research and development effort and instead had allowed private spending its head; or that bright people with advanced professional training would be more plentiful if education had been rationed by a full-cost price.

The truth is that modern science has made public the very activity of producing innovations. New knowledge has always been the purest of public goods, but as long as its "production" did not require systematic commitment of substantial resources beyond the time and energy of self-motivated individuals, such production was relatively insensitive to considerations of profit. But today, research (and development) is a costly as well as risky big business; it takes massive application of expensive resources. And precisely because the "output" of such activity has a strong public quality, markets cannot be counted on to produce enough of it.[10]

Efficiency and Choice of Institutions

If, then, people care for goods and services with strong public quality, *and if their tastes matter,* the case against markets stands—"local" inefficiency, tax distortion, and dynamics notwithstanding. The rule that allocation by markets cannot be improved upon, that shifting of resources from government to private use will necessarily improve allocation, is—or ought to be—dead. The truth is that it is all too easy to overuse markets, and at grave cost.

But if the old rule is dead, what is to take its place? How, if we cannot trust to markets, are we to decide how to divide our means between roads and automobile assemblies, between schools and hospitals and private consumables? Just what in-

[10] Moreover, where research does yield private profit, where "appropriation" is feasible, the fruit of such research, new communicable knowledge, will be badly underused. Rationing of knowledge by price is as inefficient as is the rationing of any public good by price. But, in fact, appropriation is often difficult, usable results always uncertain, and hence private risk is anyway apt to be higher than true social risk.

It does not follow, of course, that for fast economic growth we must have a $40 billion defense program. What does follow is that, if the Russians should call it quits tomorrow and if a fast-growing GNP still were to matter, then it might make sense to redirect and even step up rather than scale down government spending for research and development, not to speak of education. This would be so even if we were all to agree that we would use increases in productivity to permit more leisure and to improve the quality of life in more subtle ways than by producing bigger cars.

stitutional machinery will keep us from going wrong?

It is beyond the scope of this essay to explore these difficult and largely unanswered questions about the theory and practice of political decision making. Anyone who has thought through the logic of the public-good phenomenon will have a fair idea about what is involved. Suffice it only to point out that:

1. None of the above implies that we ought to abandon private market choice over all decreasing-cost/public-good activities. In fact, we have evidently not done so. Economies of scale preclude anything like pure competition in most of basic industry (e.g., metals, machinery, chemicals, automobiles); yet apart from antitrust supervision we tend to leave well enough alone. And wisely so. With political procedures for getting people to reveal their tastes and for inducing governments to act on these as cumbersome as they are, it makes eminent sense to use markets wherever profit-guided allocation can be counted on not to go too wrong. "Workable competition," in all its fuzziness, is the appropriate notion.[11]

But one must not go too far. There is no escaping the need for community-wide allocation decisions. True, imperfect markets are likely to do better than imperfect government by many decreasing-cost activities. But which many? The very decision of what is and is not too wrong implies collective matching of costs against benefits. Moreover, it is evident that as concerns a wide variety of activities market allocation will in fact be too wrong to suffer.

2. On the other hand, even where "free" markets do very badly, public spending is not necessarily the right or only medicine. One has only to look about, at education, transport,

[11] Anyone who doubts that political and administrative procedures are exceedingly clumsy in mediating production and distribution according to people's tastes should think about what would happen if supply and distribution on the island of Manhattan had to be organized without resort to markets.

insurance, public health, research, etc., to realize how varied is the store of organizational devices and instrumentalities available to us for blending various kinds of private and public action, and how rich the possibilities for constructive social invention. Choice, happily, is not confined to the polar extremes of "free" markets and public spending with free distribution.[12]

3. Nonetheless, public spending will have an important place; hence it is important that it not be governed by misleading rules. Dicta such as that if defense spending goes up, nondefense public spending must come down; that because public spending involves a lot of waste it ought to be cut; that it is better to counter recession by inducing private spending via tax cuts than by increasing public spending; that if spending by government is increased in recession, it ought to finance short-lived projects—are, as simple-minded rules often are, arbitrary and, if people's tastes matter, wrong. They are corollaries of the erroneous proposition that private market choices

[12] One reason why it is inexcusable, even on the level of strategy, to permit considerations of operating inefficiency and waste to mask the more fundamental and difficult questions about the gross scale of public activities is precisely that central political decision about scale does not preclude either decentralized administration and operation of a particular activity or the enlistment via appropriate incentive schemes of private energies to reduce operating inefficiency and stimulate imaginative innovation. The real issue as regards the organization of education, for instance, is not whether it ought to be public or private, but what mix of institutional devices involving private, local, state, and federal action will do reasonably well given that (1) the benefits of education are partially public not only as between individuals but also as between different localities and different states—improved education of young Kentuckians is of benefit to the community of Americans living outside of Kentucky: I care about the intelligence of the Kentucky electorate, and, more generally, about physicists and doctors trained outside of my school district; (2) local operation and administration of schools has important efficiency advantages; (3) private schools may be more independent of some kinds of political pressure than public, and hence may more easily afford imagination and courage.

are necessarily more efficient in catering to people's tastes than communal choices.[13]

4. Again, of course, it is easier to point out what is wrong with bad rules than to suggest good ones. The fact is that neither in political theory nor in political practice have we made much progress with the problem of how, in David Riesman's phrase, to "institutionalize our collective aspirations"—or, more precisely, our individual aspirations for intrinsically collective goods and services. This is not surprising. As concerns theory, whatever exploratory work has been done suggests that general solutions will not be easy to come by. And as concerns practice, there is much in the American tradition to make us rather less ingenious in tackling this range of problems—rather more prone to dogma and less inclined to pragmatic experimentation—than has been our wont in responding to challenges more peremptory and more susceptible to once-for-all solutions. Yet on the level of strategy, at least, it is not difficult to think of ground rules which might help us do a lot better than we have been doing. Perhaps the most important of these, which underlies all the others, is that our political leaders,

[13] One such rule—that any shift of responsibility for public activities from Washington to state-local governments is good, and that the reverse is bad—warrants special comment. The case is usually put in terms of administrative efficiency, responsiveness to what people really want, etc. As regards decisions about the allocation of funds to activities that are "public" as between different states (e.g., conservation, roads, and, to a point, education) the argument is obviously faulty. But one has to be careful even as regards activities which do not strongly affect people in other states and localities. Provision by the federal government of free public services in Alabama is one way of redistributing real income from taxpayers in general to people in Alabama, and hence federal expenditure on what looks like narrowly intrastate functions must in part be evaluated in terms of its effect on the distribution of income. The issue cannot be settled in terms of "local" efficiency but must take into account the ethical and political considerations which are implicit in any judgment about income distribution. (This would be the case even if there were no obstacles to serious tax reform at the state and local level.)

at all levels and of both parties, explicitly acknowledge and debate the true economic choices involved in allocation for what they really are—choices about how to divide up our scarce resources among various public and private activities. Indeed, it is hardly an overstatement that honest and detailed specification of the choices we face as a community in the use of our resources is one of the most important responsibilities of political leadership. People cannot be expected to set out these choices by themselves; hence if questions of "local" inefficiency, inflation, and spurious rules about what we can afford are not to foreclose explicit consideration of how the extra billion dollars had best be used, people in positions of trust, influence, and power must help do the job. The more so since the fiction of given preferences *is* a fiction—people's preferences are sensitive to their perception of alternatives—and unless the communal stake in defense, foreign aid, public health, pure research, education, urban renewal, and the like is articulated with precision and force, our taste for "private" things, which do not lack for articulators, is likely to dominate.

This, then, is where one ends up if one cares about people's tastes—or, in truth, if one cares about the quality of life in an increasingly crowded United States. And this, too, is the proper setting for any serious discussion of the role of public spending, no matter how much one cares about political freedom. Daydreaming about how nice it would be if allocation by markets were as costless in the sphere of "public" as in the sphere of private activities is of no use. We must face up to the dilemmas of social organization posed by the need for communal allocation, and, in particular, to the conflicts, if any, between communal allocation and freedom.

8 NOTES ON ECONOMICS, POLITICS, AND FREEDOM

THE libertarian assertion that "the alternative to the invisible hand is the mailed fist of government" is a truism. But slogans are not designed for close reading; what is meant, no doubt, is that allocation through government spending, *in contrast with allocation by markets,* involves coercion and hence is inimical to liberty.

What are the effects of government taxing and spending on freedom? More generally, what are the links between market allocation and individual liberties? This is not the place to attempt even cursory discussion of these, the grand questions of political economy.[1] I should like only to comment briefly on some relevant issues of logic:

1. The view that allocation by markets involves no coercion, i.e., no restriction of freedom, hardly warrants mention. Freedom, in its most general sense, is simply "absence of obstacles to the realization of desires" (B. Russell). Even if we mean by

[1] Of all the vast literature, suffice it to cite, as a recent contribution, Isaiah Berlin's inaugural lecture as Chichele Professor at Oxford (*Two Concepts of Liberty,* Oxford, 1958). I should like to mention also an unpublished essay by Paul Samuelson entitled "Politics, Ethics, and Economics," the reading of which, some years ago, greatly benefited my thinking on these matters.

obstacles only those due to the actions of other human beings (thereby absolving the law of gravity), it is evident that the fact of scarcity relative to wants implies coercion no matter by what institutional devices we choose to parcel out apples and nuts amongst people. Laissez-faire markets, as also well-policed competitive markets, constitute a particular political structure, with a particular set of rules and practices, which yields a particular distribution of the things people want. And though coercion is relatively implicit, to deny that it exists is to imply not only that a regime of free markets is God-ordained but also that it is not subject to alteration by sinful men.

2. In distribution, mandatory decision through political processes is inescapable. But does not government purchase of goods and services result in further, avoidable coercion? Once the distribution of income is fixed, either implicitly by adoption of a particular organizational scheme or explicitly by means of tax-transfer arrangements, a market system allows everyone "free" choice in how to use his own share. Market allocations as between caviar and shoes are, it appears, uncoerced. In contrast, government purchases, sanctioned albeit indirectly by majority vote, cannot avoid coercing at least the taxpaying minority who vote nay. Therefore, it is argued, to avoid unnecessary coercion, use markets.

This would be fine, or almost so, *if it were not for public goods*. The argument fails to take into account the all-or-none and for-all-or-for-none aspects of choice where public-good/decreasing-cost phenomena are involved. There is no way of having more national defense for me without having more for you; and if X and Y, in the majority, vote against more defense—or block recourse to extra-market political procedures—while Z is eager for more defense, the outcome is hardly free of coercion. Z, it is true, is free to spend his money on "freely" chosen private things, but he is not free to "buy" a $300 share of a billion dollars' worth of extra defense, or of a $10,000 mosquito control program, or of a playground for his children.[2]

The mistake lies in blaming the *procedure* of choice—voting, when in fact it is the all-or-none element in the choice itself that is to blame. If all goods were private and finely divisible, governmental allocation by vote would not have to override minorities any more (or less) than would markets; with proportional representation voting everyone could get exactly what he voted for, limited only by the number of votes he was awarded to start off with.[3] But all goods are not private, and rigidly to impose free-market rules in a world full of public goods would be to deny not only minorities but also majorities the freedom to allocate resources to what they will.[4]

[2] Nor, of course, will programs of voluntary contribution do. For the reasons, see pp. 96-98.

[3] This is not to gainsay that everyone would end up with far less than if allocation were by markets (with corresponding distribution); in a world with only private goods, markets would be incomparably more efficient than the political process. But the difference lies in organizational efficiency and not the extent of coercion in allocation.

[4] It should be pointed out that the separation of "distribution" from "allocation" (as made in the text) involves a measure of sleight of hand, and that in a deeper sense competitive markets (and also voting) are necessarily coercive in allocation as well as in distribution even as regards private goods. The distribution of "real" income as between, say, a gourmet and a dandy depends not only on the distribution of dollar income but also on the price of roast beef and the price of silk shirts. Prices, in turn, depend on how the rest of us divide *our* fixed dollar incomes between silk and beef. In general, if X should lose his appetite and develop a taste for silk, the price of beef would fall and that of silk would rise; hence Y, the dandy, would suffer a cut—Y's options depend on X's choices. Only in the limiting case where relative prices are unaffected by changes in demand will this not be so. (Economists will recognize in the limiting case the Ricardian one-factor model with constant returns to scale, in which prices are wholly cost-determined.)

On the other hand, one can conceive of a noncompetitive market setup that avoids coercion in allocation even as regards public goods. In an economy of perfectly discriminating monopolists, production would be fully efficient and everybody could buy just what he wanted. But to invoke perfect discrimination is to beg the problem. It implies

3. The conflict, as regards public goods, between freedom to choose in markets and freedom to get what one wants is but one of countless counter-examples to the notion that freedoms are necessarily complementary (or compatible). Publicists of the right are fond of emphasizing that our freedoms, in President Eisenhower's phrase, are a "single bundle"—as though interdependence implied complementarity. Unfortunately, it does nothing of the sort. Interaction among different people's individual freedoms is only too often one of rivalry and conflict. As with other good things in life that are scarce, choice and compromise are unavoidable. "Freedom for the pike is death for the minnows."[5]

4. The more difficult questions concern not these necessary, logical relations but the contingent *empirical* ties which link economic organization and individual liberties. That there exist such ties, and that they matter, is evident; we gauge our stake in the particular pattern of our economic institutions, with its checks and balances on the seeking of private profit and on the exercise of public power, not alone in terms of economic efficiency, or material security, or even justice, but in terms also of the negative goal we label personal liberty. The proper role of public spending cannot be settled without an assessment of its effects on freedom.

---

knowledge of all preference orderings, while the crucial game-theoretical implication of the Samuelson public-good model is that consumers will not reveal their preferences—it will pay them to cheat. Moreover, the question of who ultimately is to pay for public things would remain, to be settled coercively through the political determination of the distribution of income.

[5] Note the further analogy with conventional economic goods. The liberal rule (J. S. Mill) that everyone should be allowed to pursue his own goals his own way save only that he not frustrate others is but a variant of the efficiency rule of Chapter 6 applied to "freedom." Its limitations in resolving issues, too, are qualitatively of the same sort, if rather more severe. (I appropriated the quotation from Isaiah Berlin's above cited lecture.)

But to be dogmatic about these effects is either to be less than honest or to play the fool. There exists no general formula to inform us whether an increase in spending by government on education, health, slum-clearance, or social security will *on balance* decrease or increase freedom. Barring extreme cases, history reveals no simple patterns, certainly none that tells us much about the consequences for freedom of an increase in public purchases from a fifth to a fourth of total output. Complex variety is what strikes the eye—a variety which suggests that a pragmatic strategy based on precise thought about concrete situations and on careful and imaginative experimentation is more likely to serve the cause of liberty than rigid application of universal rules.

APPENDIX

Appendix GOVERNMENT SPENDING AND COST-PUSH INFLATION

IT WAS argued in Chapter 4 that an increase in government spending need not give rise to demand inflation; that it is possible without creating an inflationary excess of demand over supply to release additional resources for public use by means of the fiscal and monetary instruments of the Treasury and the Federal Reserve. But what of *cost-push?* Does not a shift of resources from private to public use generate (or accelerate) the wage-price "spiral" even if there is plenty of slack in the balance between total spending and supply? Is not the cost-push problem worse in a high-G economy?

The identifying symptom of cost-push inflation is a continuing rise in prices while markets for labor and goods are slack. There is inflation yet no inflationary gap, i.e., no excess of total spending over capacity. This does not imply a complete break in the chain which links the price level and the supply-demand balance; the greater the *de*flationary gap, i.e., the more people are unemployed, the shorter the work week, the more unused plant capacity there is, the less likely are bullishly inflationary wage-price bargains or privately administered price increases. But in a post-adjustment situation, at least, it is again the gap between capacity and *total* spending that matters, and not how the total is split between private and public sources. With a large enough cushion of excess capacity in labor and product markets, maintaining or even slowly increasing the share of government in a growing total should not give rise to cost-push pressures. And if the cushion is insufficient, a small ratio of G to total spending will not help.[1]

Things are much more complicated if we consider not a post-adjustment situation but the *process* of shifting resources from private to public use. The specific resources released by a tax-induced cut in private spending will not match the particular inputs for which producers will bid to supply the government's additional orders. Relative to the new pattern of demand, some things will become less scarce, other things more scarce; the balance between supply and demand in particular markets will change, and both producers and users must be induced to adjust their input-output decisions to reflect such change. If the price system is to do its bit and mediate such adjustment, the pattern of relative prices must change.

Under a regime of pure competition, the need for change in relative prices would cause little trouble. In markets with excess supply, prices would fall; where demand had increased relative to supply, prices would rise. Price indices might show movement in one direction or another, but as long as total spending and capacity were in rough balance such movement would reflect only the statistical idiosyncrasies of the indices. (The impact on income distribution of a very large change in

[1] Like all aggregative statements, this too must be qualified to take account of some compositional effects. E.g., if government orders are biased in favor of industries more oligopolistic in structure than the average of civilian suppliers, cost-push is more likely in a high-G than in a low-G situation and it would take more slack across-the-board to check it. On the other hand, labor productivity may increase faster under a high-G than a low-G regime because more of G is manufactured and less of it consists of services; this would work the other way. But at least as concerns post-adjustment situations, all such compositional effects are of second order. Moreover, one must be careful about the facts: a shift from non-G to G type manufactures may well reduce "productivity"—aircraft speedometers require much finer tolerances than Thunderbird speedometers.

relative prices might give rise to considerable pain, especially where special-purpose factors of production are involved. But for relatively small shifts in demand this is not apt to be serious; and, anyway, there are many ways of cushioning the shock.)

In less than perfectly competitive markets, however, we run into trouble. Changes in prices will only partially reflect changes in scarcities. More important from our point of view, whatever price changes do occur are likely all to be one way—up. It is a characteristic of many important markets in the United States, and not only of the organized labor market, that prices are flexible upward only. If, to secure efficient reallocation, relative prices must change, the price level itself must rise.

In itself, such a one-round increase would not be too worrisome. It would facilitate efficient reallocation, and it might even help to restrain private spending by shrinking the value of liquid balances. Any adverse effects on distribution, moreover, could easily be offset. But with the proliferation, since the war, of escalator clauses, parity arrangements, and the like, the process will not stop there. A rise in the consumer price index is itself a signal for increasing wage rates, which in turn will trigger a further cost-plus markup of prices and a further rise in the indices.

Note, however, the peculiarities of this process:

1. It is touched off by any shift in resource use substantial enough to require large price changes. Qualitatively, at least, it is not partial to a shift from private to public use; a sharp reverse shift can give rise to the same problem. (Quantitatively, it is true, the upward push is likely to be of greater intensity if induced by a shift from private to public use than for the reverse. The pressure on wage rates is apt to be greater when due to a *cut* in after-tax incomes than when contention is over how to share an *increase* in real income. Except in recession, increasing G implies decreasing real disposable income; and both wage bargains and price lists are likely to reflect an at-

tempt to push the burden onto others. This is all the more likely, given the sensitivity of our escalator arrangements to price indices, if the initial cut in real income takes the form not of an increase in personal income taxes but of a rise in prices due to excise and sales taxes or to profit taxes which are pushed forward.)

2. Nonetheless, and even during the process of adjustment, the intensity of cost-push is likely to be sensitive to the aggregate balance between spending and capacity. It does not take a large price premium to draw *idle* resources from one "use" into another; if there is enough slack, the first-round price increases are unlikely to be very large. Moreover, initial increases are less likely to trigger secondary wage-price markups; the appeal of a higher price on output that one cannot sell is hardly irresistible, especially if a rise in price is likely to lose further sales.

Cost-push inflation, if appreciable, poses a nasty dilemma. It can, no doubt, be controlled by traditional means; one can compress demand by taxes and tight money until there is enough unemployment and idle capacity to stop all price rise. Whether it is the part of wisdom to suffer the medicine is another matter. At the least, it would pay to give some hard thought to what could be done to introduce some acceptable yet noninflationary criteria into the bargaining process in markets where competition is not vigorous enough to do the job.

But as concerns the appropriate balance between private and public spending, all this is diversion. To the extent that cost-push inflation is sensitive to spending, it is the relation between *total* spending and capacity that really matters. Short of a mobilization effort, i.e., a ratio of G to GNP of 30 per cent plus, and barring only a forced draft, high-tempo shift of resources from private to public use, the split of the total between public and private sources is of secondary importance. We cannot evade the cost-push dilemma by shifting resources from public to private use.

TABLE 1 GOVERNMENT EXPENDITURE, 1929-1957[a]
(Billions of Dollars)

Year	(1) Total Government Expenditure[b c] (E)	(2) Total Government Purchases of Goods and Services (G)	(3) Total Government Non-exhaustive Expenditure[d] (N)	(4) Federal Expenditure[b c] (FE)	(5) Federal Purchases of Goods and Services (FG)
1929	10.2	8.5	1.7	2.6	1.3
1930	11.0	9.2	1.8	2.8	1.4
1931	12.3	9.2	3.1	4.2	1.5
1932	10.6	8.1	2.5	3.2	1.5
1933	10.7	8.0	2.6	4.0	2.0
1934	12.8	9.8	3.1	6.4	3.0
1935	13.3	10.0	3.4	6.5	2.9
1936	15.9	11.8	4.1	8.5	4.8
1937	14.8	11.7	3.1	7.2	4.6
1938	16.6	12.8	3.8	8.5	5.3
1939	17.5	13.3	4.2	9.0	5.2
1940	18.5	14.1	4.4	10.1	6.2
1941	28.8	24.8	4.0	20.5	16.9
1942	64.0	59.7	4.3	56.1	52.0
1943	93.4	88.6	4.8	86.0	81.2
1944	103.1	96.5	6.5	95.6	89.0
1945	92.9	82.9	10.1	84.8	74.8
1946	47.0	30.8	16.2	37.0	20.9
1947[f]	43.0	28.4	14.6	31.7	17.0
1948[f]	46.8	31.1	15.8	32.5	17.2
1949[f]	56.5	41.2	15.3	39.8	24.6
1950[f]	61.5	42.1	19.4	42.3	23.2
1951[f]	65.9	49.4	16.5	45.4	28.8
1952[f]	88.7	72.0	16.7	66.6	49.6
1953[f]	99.7	82.4	17.3	76.3	58.5
1954[f]	99.9	81.3	18.7	74.4	55.2
1955[f]	96.8	75.8	21.0	68.2	46.6
1956[f]	100.6	78.1	22.6	69.8	46.5
1957[f]	110.1	84.5	25.5	76.3	49.6

SOURCES: Purchases of Goods and Services, 1929-1946 and Fiscal 1947-1957: *Survey of Current Business,* July, 1958. Total and Nonexhaustive Expenditures, Calendar 1929-1945: *Supplement to Survey of Current Business,* 1954. Total and Nonexhaustive Expenditures, Calendar 1946 and Fiscal 1947-1957: *U.S. Income and Output (1958 Supplement to the Survey of Current Business),* U.S. Department of Commerce (see, however, note [d]).

NOTE: Components will not necessarily add to totals because of rounding.

[a] 1929-1946 stand for calendar years; 1947-1957 for fiscal years (f).

(6) Federal Non-exhaustive Expenditure[d] (FN)	(7) State and Local Government Expenditure[bc] (SE)	(8) State and Local Government Purchases of Goods and Services (SG)	(9) State and Local Government Non-exhaustive Expenditure[d] (SN)	(10) Gross National Product (GNP)
1.3	7.7	7.2	.5	104.4
1.4	8.4	7.8	.6	91.1
2.6	8.4	7.7	.8	76.3
1.7	7.6	6.6	1.0	58.5
2.0	7.2	6.0	1.2	56.0
3.4	8.1	6.8	1.3	65.0
3.6	8.5	7.1	1.5	72.5
3.7	8.1	7.0	1.1	82.7
2.7	8.4	7.2	1.2	90.8
3.2	8.9	7.5	1.4	85.2
3.8	9.6	8.2	1.4	91.1
3.9	9.2	7.9	1.3	100.6
3.6	9.0	7.8	1.2	125.8
4.1	8.8	7.7	1.1	159.1
4.7	8.4	7.4	1.0	192.5
6.6	8.4	7.5	.9	211.4
10.0	9.0	8.1	.9	213.6
16.1	11.1	9.9	1.2	210.7
14.7	12.8	11.4	1.4	223.6
15.4	16.1	13.9	2.2	247.0
15.2	18.8	16.6	2.2	261.5
19.1	21.6	18.9	2.7	264.0
16.5	23.0	20.7	2.4	310.4
17.1	24.6	22.4	2.2	338.6
17.8	26.2	23.9	2.2	359.7
19.2	28.4	26.1	2.3	361.8
21.6	31.6	29.2	2.4	377.5
23.3	33.9	31.6	2.4	409.5
26.7	37.4	34.9	2.5	432.1

[b] As shown in the national income accounts. These, "like the cash budget, include the transactions of the trust accounts. Unlike both the conventional budget and the cash statement, they exclude certain capital and lending transactions. In general, they do not use the cash basis for transactions with business. Instead, . . . expenditures are timed with the delivery instead of the payment for goods and services; and CCC guaranteed price-support crop loans financed by banks are counted as expenditures when the loans are made, not when CCC redeems them."

(*Continued.*)

[c] Total government expenditure (E) is less than the sum of federal expenditures (FE) and state-local expenditures (SE) by the amount of federal grants-in-aid to state and local governments. (These last are intragovernmental transactions for all governments taken together.)

[d] N is less than the sum of FN and SN by the amount of federal grants-in-aid to state and local governments (as per Column 2 of Table 2). Also N and FN differ from the revised Department of Commerce series to be found in *U.S. Income and Output* (1958) in that they do not include "net foreign transfers." Such transfers to foreigners (under various aid programs) are here treated as government purchases of goods and services. (This corresponds to earlier Commerce Department practice, as, for instance, in the July 1958 issue of the *Survey of Current Business* which contains series for purchases of goods and services that are revised but include "foreign transfers".)

TABLE 2 COMPOSITION OF NONEXHAUSTIVE GOVERNMENT EXPENDITURE, 1929-1957[a]
(Billions of Dollars)

Year	(1) Federal Transfer Payments[c]	(2) Federal Grants-in-aid to State and Local Gov'ts	(3) Federal Net Interest Paid	(4) Federal Subsidies Less Surplus of Gov't Enterprises	(5) Federal Non-exhaustive Expenditure (Sum of 1+2+3+4)[b c] (FN)	(6) State and Local Transfer Payments
1929	.7	.1	.4	.1	1.3	.2
1930	.7	.1	.4	.1	1.4	.3
1931	1.7	.3	.4	.2	2.6	.3
1932	.9	.1	.5	.2	1.7	.5
1933	.7	.5	.5	.3	2.0	.8
1934	.6	1.6	.6	.6	3.4	1.0
1935	.6	1.7	.5	.7	3.6	1.2
1936	2.1	.7	.5	.4	3.7	.9
1937	.8	.8	.6	.5	2.7	1.0
1938	1.2	.8	.6	.6	3.2	1.2
1939	1.2	1.0	.6	.9	3.8	1.3
1940	1.4	.9	.7	.9	3.9	1.3
1941	1.4	.8	.8	.7	3.6	1.2
1942	1.4	.9	1.0	.8	4.1	1.2
1943	1.2	.9	1.7	.9	4.7	1.2
1944	1.8	.9	2.4	1.4	6.6	1.2
1945	4.3	.9	3.3	1.5	10.0	1.3
1946	9.2	1.1	4.2	1.6	16.1	1.6
1947[f]	8.2	1.5	4.2	.8	14.7	1.9
1948[f]	8.8	1.8	4.2	.6	15.4	2.8
1949[f]	8.1	2.1	4.4	.7	15.2	2.8
1950[f]	11.3	2.4	4.5	1.0	19.1	3.3
1951[f]	8.3	2.4	4.6	1.3	16.5	3.1
1952[f]	8.7	2.5	4.8	1.2	17.1	3.0
1953[f]	9.4	2.8	4.8	.9	17.8	3.2
1954[f]	10.5	2.8	5.0	.9	19.2	3.3
1955[f]	12.3	2.9	5.0	1.4	21.6	3.5
1956[f]	12.9	3.1	5.0	2.2	23.3	3.6
1957[f]	14.6	3.6	5.5	3.0	26.7	3.8

SOURCES: 1929-1945: *Supplement to Survey of Current Business,* 1954. Calendar 1946 and Fiscal 1947-1957: *U.S. Income and Output,* 1958.

[a] 1929-1946 stand for calendar years; 1947-1957 for fiscal years (f).

[b] Components will not necessarily add to totals because of rounding.

[c] Federal transfers (and hence federal nonexhaustive expenditure) do not include "net foreign transfers." For reasons, see note [d], Table 1.

(7) State and Local Net Interest Paid	(8) Current Deficit of State and Local Government Enterprises	(9) State and Local Gov't Non-exhaustive Expenditure (Sum of 6+7+8)[b] (SN)	(10) Total Gov't Transfer Payments (Sum of 1+6)	(11) Total Gov't Interest Paid (Sum of 3+7)	(12) Total Subsidies Less Surplus of Gov't Enterprises (Sum of 4+8)	(13) National Income[d]
.5	−.2	.5	.9	.9	−.1	87.8
.6	−.2	.6	1.0	1.0	−.1	75.7
.6	−.2	.8	2.0	1.0	0	59.7
.7	−.2	1.0	1.4	1.2	0	42.5
.7	−.2	1.2	1.5	1.2	.1	40.2
.6	−.3	1.3	1.6	1.2	.3	49.0
.6	−.3	1.5	1.8	1.1	.4	57.1
.6	−.4	1.1	3.0	1.1	0	64.9
.6	−.4	1.2	1.8	1.2	.1	73.6
.6	−.4	1.4	2.4	1.2	.2	67.6
.6	−.4	1.4	2.5	1.2	.5	72.8
.6	−.5	1.3	2.7	1.3	.4	81.6
.5	−.6	1.2	2.6	1.3	.1	104.7
.5	−.6	1.1	2.6	1.5	.2	137.7
.4	−.7	1.0	2.4	2.1	.2	170.3
.4	−.7	.9	3.0	2.8	.7	182.6
.3	−.8	.9	5.6	3.6	.7	181.2
.3	−.8	1.2	10.8	4.5	.8	180.9
.3	−.8	1.4	10.1	4.5	0	191.2
.3	−.8	2.2	11.6	4.5	−.2	210.5
.3	−.9	2.2	10.8	4.7	−.2	223.7
.3	−.9	2.7	14.6	4.8	.1	222.1
.3	−1.0	2.4	11.4	4.9	.3	265.2
.3	−1.2	2.2	11.7	5.1	0	285.8
.3	−1.2	2.2	12.6	5.1	−.3	302.0
.4	−1.4	2.3	13.8	5.4	−.5	301.5
.4	−1.5	2.4	15.8	5.4	−.1	313.2
.5	−1.7	2.4	16.5	5.5	.5	341.2
.5	−1.8	2.5	18.4	6.0	1.2	358.6

[d] National Income equals GNP *less* capital consumption allowances, indirect business tax and nontax liability, business transfer payments, statistical discrepancy, *plus* subsidies less surplus of government enterprises. It is the sum total of compensation of employees, proprietors' income, rental income of persons, corporate profits and inventory valuation adjustment, and net interest.

TABLE 3 TOTAL AND PER CAPITA GROSS NATIONAL PRODUCT AND GOVERNMENT PURCHASES OF GOODS AND SERVICES IN 1957 DOLLARS, 1929-1957[a]

Year	(1) Total Gov't Purchases of Goods and Services* (Billions of 1957 Dollars) (G*)	(2) Federal Purchases of Goods and Services* (Billions of 1957 Dollars) (FG*)	(3) State and Local Purchases of Goods and Services* (Billions of 1957 Dollars) (SG*)	(4) Population[b] (Millions) (P)	(5) Households[d] (Millions) (H)	(6) Per Capita Gov't Purchases of Goods and Services* (1957 Dollars) G*/P
1929	20.6	3.3	17.2	121.9	30.1	169
1930	22.7	3.8	18.8	123.2	30.6	185
1931	24.0	4.1	19.7	124.1	31.0	193
1932	22.8	4.3	18.3	124.9	31.4	182
1933	22.2	5.9	16.1	125.7	31.7	176
1934	25.3	7.8	17.4	126.5	32.0	200
1935	25.6	7.5	17.9	127.4	32.4	201
1936	29.9	11.5	18.3	128.2	32.8	233
1937	28.9	10.8	18.0	129.0	33.1	224
1938	32.0	12.8	19.1	130.0	33.5	246
1939	33.5	12.3	21.0	131.0	n.a.	256
1940	34.6	14.7	19.8	132.1	34.9	262
1941	53.0	34.4	18.7	133.4	35.9	397
1942	111.4	94.9	16.9	134.9	36.4	826
1943	153.2	138.6	15.4	136.7	36.9	1,121
1944	169.3	155.0	15.2	138.4	37.1	1,223
1945	145.8	131.0	15.5	139.9	37.5	1,042
1946	49.4	32.1	17.3	141.4	38.2	349
$(1947)^{cal.}$	(41.5)	(21.9)	(19.6)	(144.1)		(288)
1947^{f}	42.8	24.1	18.5	142.8	39.1	300
1948^{f}	43.9	23.4	20.3	145.5	40.7	302
1949^{f}	54.4	31.9	22.4	148.0	42.1	368
1950^{f}	54.9	29.3	25.4	150.6	43.5	364
1951^{f}	60.1	33.9	26.1	153.1	44.7	392
1952^{f}	82.8	56.2	26.6	155.8	45.5	531
1953^{f}	93.0	65.8	27.3	158.4	46.3	587
1954^{f}	91.6	62.5	29.2	161.1	46.9	569
1955^{f}	83.0	51.3	31.8	164.0	47.8	506
1956^{f}	82.2	48.9	33.3	166.8	48.8	493
1957^{f}	84.5	49.6	34.9	169.8	49.5	498

NOTE: Components will not necessarily add to totals because of rounding.
* Implicit price deflators for $1929^{cal.}$-$1947^{cal.}$ are those of the Department of Commerce (*U.S. Income and Output*, 1948) adjusted to a base of 1957^{f}= 100. The 1948^{f}-1957^{f} deflators, in turn, are based on the Commerce Department's *quarterly* series *(ibid.)*. Since the Commerce quarterly series only

(7) Per Capita Federal Purchases of Goods and Services* (1957 Dollars) FG*/P	(8) Per Household Gov't Purchases of Goods and Services* (1957 Dollars) G*/H	(9) Gross National Product* (Billions of 1957 Dollars) GNP*	(10) Per Capita Gross National Product* (1957 Dollars) GNP*/P	(11) Per Household Gross National Product* (1957 Dollars) GNP*/H	(12) Ratio of Government Purchases to GNP[d] (Per Cent) G/GNP[e]
27	684	193.5	1,587	6,427	8.1
31	743	174.9	1,419	5,714	10.1
33	774	162.5	1,309	5,242	12.1
35	726	138.5	1,108	4,409	13.8
47	699	134.6	1,071	4,247	14.3
61	791	147.3	1,165	4,603	15.1
59	790	162.6	1,277	5,020	13.8
90	910	184.4	1,439	5,623	14.3
84	872	195.0	1,512	5,891	12.9
99	956	186.1	1,432	5,554	15.0
94	n.a.	201.4	1,537	n.a.	14.6
111	992	218.8	1,656	6,269	14.0
258	1,477	252.9	1,896	7,044	19.7
703	3,060	283.9	2,105	7,799	37.5
1,014	4,152	315.4	2,307	8,547	46.0
1,120	4,563	338.0	2,442	9,110	45.6
936	3,887	333.9	2,386	8,905	38.8
227	1,292	300.3	2,124	7,860	14.6
(152)		(300.1)	(2,082)		(12.2)
169	1,095	299.8	2,099	7,668	12.7
161	1,078	305.6	2,101	7,509	12.6
216	1,292	312.2	2,110	7,416	15.8
194	1,261	319.0	2,119	7,333	15.9
222	1,344	353.8	2,311	7,915	15.9
361	1,819	369.3	2,371	8,117	21.3
415	2,009	387.3	2,445	8,365	22.9
388	1,954	386.5	2,399	8,241	22.5
313	1,737	399.8	2,438	8,363	20.1
293	1,685	425.0	2,548	8,709	19.1
292	1,708	432.1	2,545	8,730	19.6

cover the last two quarters of fiscal 1947, the indices for that year are composite, based on the Commerce figures for the last two quarters and on quarter-by-quarter projections of these back into the first two quarters of fiscal 1947. The rates of projection were derived from the (monthly) consumer price index for "all commodities." (*Survey of Current Business,* Sept., 1949.)

(*Continued.*)

[a] 1929-1947[cal.] stand for calendar years; 1947[f]-1957[f] for fiscal years.

[b] The population figures are for the continental United States including armed forces overseas. For *calendar* 1929-1947, they are as of July 1 (Table 2, *Statistical Abstract of the U.S.*, 1958, p. 5, except for 1929 which is from the *Economic Report of the President,* 1958, p. 131). For *fiscal* 1947-1957 the figures are as of January 1. (*Current Population Reports,* Department of Commerce, Series P-25, No. 71, April 3, 1953 and No. 205, September 11, 1959.)

[d] The 1929-1938 household figures were estimated from the series for "Families" given in *Economic Almanac* 1940 (p. 50); the 1940-1949 figures are from the *Statistical Abstract* 1950 (p. 23); those for 1950-1956, from *Statistical Abstract* 1957 (p. 45).

[e] The ratio of two *undeflated* figures is a better indicator of what is wanted than the ratio of deflated figures.

TABLE 4 NONDEFENSE MAGNITUDES, 1929, 1939-1957[a]

Year	(1) Total Gov't National Security Purchases[b] (Billions of Dollars)	(2) Deflated Total National Security Purchases*[d] (Billions of 1957 Dollars)	(3) All-Government Nondefense Purchases of Goods and Services* (Billions of 1957 Dollars)	(4) Per Capita Gov't Nondefense Purchases* (1957 Dollars)
	(TNS)	(TNS)*	(G*-TNS*)	(G*-TNS*)/P
1929 est.	.7	1.7	18.9	155
1939	1.3	3.0	30.5	233
1940	2.2	5.3	29.3	222
1941	13.8	28.0	25.1	188
1942	49.4	90.0	21.4	158
1943	79.8	136.1	17.1	125
1944	87.5	152.3	17.0	123
1945	73.8	129.3	16.5	118
1946	18.7	28.7	20.7	146
(1947) cal.	(12.3)	(17.1)	(24.4)	(169)
1947f	14.1	20.1	22.7	159
1948f	13.0	17.7	26.2	180
1949f	18.2	23.6	30.8	208
1950f	17.7	22.4	32.5	216
1951f	25.3	29.8	30.3	198
1952f	44.7	50.8	32.0	206
1953f	51.3	57.7	35.3	223
1954f	47.4	53.7	37.9	236
1955f	41.0	45.1	37.9	231
1956f	40.9	42.9	39.3	236
1957f	44.8	44.8	39.8	234

[a] 1929 and 1939-1947cal. stand for calendar years; 1947f-1957f stand for fiscal years (f).

[b] The Commerce Department's "national security" category, on which the TNS series is based, is only published *gross* of government sales, and is not comparable to the Commerce series on FG, G, and GNP, all of which are *net* of government sales. Hence in order to get meaningful figures for non-defense purchases, one cannot simply subtract Commerce's "national security" component of federal purchases from total FG. (For years when government sales were high, e.g., 1945 and 1946, the residual would be negative.) Rather, it is necessary to get figures for "national security" *net* of sales of

(5)	(6)	(7)	(8)
Nondefense GNP* (Billions of 1957 Dollars)	Per Capita Nondefense GNP* (1957 Dollars)	Per Household Nondefense GNP* (1957 Dollars)	Ratio of Gov't Nondefense Purchases to Nondefense GNP (Per Cent)
GNP*-TNS*	GNP*-TNS* /P	GNP*-TNS* /H	G-TNS / GNP-TNS
191.7	1,573	6,370	7.5
198.4	1,514	n.a.	13.4
213.5	1,616	6,117	12.0
224.9	1,686	6,266	9.8
193.9	1,438	5,326	9.4
179.3	1,317	4,859	7.9
185.7	1,342	5,005	7.3
204.6	1,462	5,457	6.5
271.5	1,921	7,108	6.3
(283.1)	(1,964)		(7.3)
279.7	1,958	7,154	6.9
288.0	1,980	7,075	7.7
288.7	1,950	6,857	9.5
296.6	1,970	6,818	9.9
324.0	2,117	7,248	8.4
318.6	2,045	7,002	9.3
329.6	2,080	7,118	10.1
332.8	2,066	7,096	10.8
354.6	2,163	7,419	10.3
382.1	2,290	7,829	10.1
387.4	2,281	7,826	10.3

defense items. Unfortunately, there is no published breakdown of government sales by function; to obtain a series on "defense sales" it was assumed that "defense sales" in any year were in the same proportion to total government sales as were "national security" purchases (gross of sales) to total federal purchases gross of sales. TNS here is equal to the commerce series on "national security" purchases less the so-obtained figures for "national defense" sales.

[d] For want of a better index, TNS is deflated by the same deflator as was used for FG. The only justification for this procedure is that TNS constitutes a very large fraction of FG.

Table 5 Federal Nondefense Magnitudes, 1929, 1939-1957[a]

Year	(1) Federal Nondefense Purchases of Goods and Services (Billions of Dollars) FG-TNS[b]	(2) All-Government Nondefense Purchases of Goods and Services (Billions of Dollars) G-TNS[b]	(3) Nondefense GNP (Billions of Dollars) GNP-TNS[b]
1929 est.	.6	7.8	103.8
1939	3.9	12.1	89.8
1940	4.0	11.9	98.4
1941	3.2	11.0	112.1
1942	2.7	10.3	109.8
1943	1.5	8.9	112.8
1944	1.5	9.1	123.9
1945	1.0	9.1	139.8
1946	2.2	12.1	191.9
(1947) cal.	(3.5)	(16.2)	(222.0)
1947f	2.9	14.4	209.5
1948f	4.2	18.1	234.0
1949f	6.5	23.1	243.4
1950f	5.5	24.4	246.3
1951f	3.5	24.1	285.1
1952f	4.8	27.3	293.8
1953f	7.2	31.1	308.5
1954f	7.8	33.9	314.4
1955f	5.6	34.8	336.5
1956f	5.7	37.2	368.7
1957f	4.9	39.8	387.4

[a] 1929, 1939-1947 cal. stand for calendar years; 1947f-1957f for fiscal years (f). For sources, see basic series and previous tables.

(4) Ratio of Federal Nondefense to All-Gov't Nondefense Purchases (Per Cent) FG-TNS/ G-TNS[b]	(5) Ratio of Federal Nondefense Purchases to Nondefense GNP (Per Cent) FG-TNS/ GNP-TNS[b]	(6) Federal Nondefense Purchases of Goods and Services* (Billions of 1957 Dollars) FG*-TNS*[b]	(7) Per Capita Federal Nondefense Purchases* (1957 Dollars) FG*-TNS*[b] /P
8.1	.6	1.6	13
32.3	4.3	9.3	71
33.3	4.0	9.4	71
28.8	2.8	6.4	48
25.7	2.4	4.8	36
16.6	1.3	2.5	18
16.9	1.2	2.7	19
11.0	.7	1.8	13
18.0	1.1	3.3	24
(21.4)	(1.6)	(4.8)	(33)
19.8	1.4	4.0	28
23.3	1.8	5.8	40
28.0	2.7	8.4	56
22.5	2.2	6.9	46
14.4	1.2	4.1	27
17.7	1.6	5.5	35
23.1	2.3	8.1	51
23.0	2.5	8.8	55
16.1	1.7	6.2	38
15.2	1.5	6.0	36
12.2	1.3	4.9	29

[b] Recall that TNS is net of sales, as are G, FG, and GNP (see note b, Table 4).

TABLE 6 GOVERNMENT PURCHASES OF GOODS AND SERVICES BY TYPE OF FUNCTION, CALENDAR 1957

(Millions of Dollars)

	Federal Purchases of Goods and Services FG	Sate and Local Purchases of Goods and Services SG	All-Government Purchases of Goods and Services G
Total	50,832[a]	36,300	87,132[a]
NATIONAL DEFENSE	44,347	204	44,551
Military services and foreign military assistance	41,574	69	41,643
Atomic energy development	2,024	97	2,121
Stockpiling and defense facilities	567	—	567
Other	182	38	220
GENERAL GOVERNMENT	1,378	3,404	4,782
General administration	809	1,735	2,544
General property and records management	202	367	569
Central personnel management and employment costs	312	1,156	1,468
Other	55	146	201
INTERNATIONAL AFFAIRS AND FINANCE	2,068[a]	—	2,068[a]
Conduct of foreign affairs and informational activities	300	—	300
Foreign economic assistance	1,768[a]	—	1,768[a]
HEALTH, EDUCATION, AND WELFARE	722	21,745	22,467
Public health and sanitation	265	4,584	4,849
Education	108	13,506	13,614
Elementary and secondary	{63} (Elementary and secondary and Higher)	11,320	{13,095} (Elementary and secondary and Higher)
Higher		1,712	
Other	45	474	519
Social security and special welfare services	260	635	895
Public assistance and relief	2	635	637
Old age and retirement benefits	161	—	161
Other	97	—	97
Civilian safety	27	2,772	2,799
Police	—	1,454	1,454
Fire	—	800	800
Prisons	27	518	545
Labor and manpower	51	248	299
Other	11	—	11

	Federal Purchases of Goods and Services FG	Sate and Local Purchases of Goods and Services SG	All-Government Purchases of Goods and Services G
VETERANS' SERVICES AND BENEFITS	1,006	10	1,016
Education, training, and other benefits	9	—	9
Hospitals and medical care	813	—	813
Administration and other services	184	10	194
COMMERCE AND HOUSING	506	9,350	9,856
Regulation of commerce and finance	47	506	553
Transportation	362	7,398	7,760
Highways	35	7,187	7,222
Water	119	101	220
Air	208	110	318
Housing and community redevelopment	9	176	185
Public utilities	—	1,206	1,206
Transit	—	117	117
Electricity	—	327	327
Water and gas	—	762	762
Postal services	47	—	47
Other	41	64	105
AGRICULTURE AND AGRICULTURAL RESOURCES	−208	469	261
Stabilization of farm prices and income	−544	—	−544
Financing farm ownership and utilities	31	—	31
Conservation of agricultural resources	117	469	586
Other services	188	—	188
NATURAL RESOURCES	1,435	1,118	2,553
Conservation and development of resources	1,330	559	1,889
Recreational use of natural resources	63	559	622
Other	42	—	42
LESS: GOVERNMENT SALES	422		422

SOURCE: *U.S. Income and Output,* 1958.
[a] Adjusted to include "foreign transfers," as per Note [d], Table 1.

TABLE 7 GOVERNMENT PURCHASES OF GOODS AND SERVICES BY FUNCTION, FISCAL 1947-1957
(Billions of Dollars)

Year	(1) Major National Security Less Defense Support			(2) International Affairs Plus Defense Support			(3) Economic Aid[a]			(4) Veterans' Services and Benefits			(5) Labor and Welfare			(6) Agriculture		
	Fed.	Total	S&L	Fed.	Total	S&L	Fed.	Total	S&L	Fed.	Total	S&L	Fed.	Total	S&L	Fed.	Total	S&L
1947	11.8	11.8	—	2.1	2.1	—	n.a.	n.a.	—	1.9	n.a.	n.a.	.3	n.a.	n.a.	−.2	n.a.	n.a.
1948	11.2	11.2	—	2.4	2.4	—	n.a.	n.a.	—	1.5	n.a.	n.a.	.3	8.7	8.4	.5	.7	.2
1949	12.6	12.6	—	5.3	5.3	—	n.a.	n.a.	—	1.5	n.a.	n.a.	.3	n.a.	n.a.	2.3	n.a.	n.a.
1950	12.8	12.8	—	4.5	4.5	—	n.a.	n.a.	—	1.8	n.a.	n.a.	.4	11.5	11.1	1.1	1.3	.2
1951	22.1	22.1	—	3.5	3.5	—	n.a.	n.a.	—	1.2	n.a.	n.a.	.4	n.a.	n.a.	−1.1	n.a.	n.a.
1952	43.5	43.5	—	2.4	2.4	—	.2	.2	—	1.4	1.5	.1	.4	13.2	12.8	−.2	.1	.3
1953	49.3	49.3	—	2.0	2.0	—	.2	.2	—	1.1	1.2	.1	.4	14.4	14.0	2.3	2.6	.3
1954	46.2	46.2	—	1.6	1.6	—	.4	.4	—	1.1	1.2	.1	.4	16.0	15.6	3.0	3.3	.3
1955	39.8	39.8	—	2.1	2.1	—	.4	.4	—	1.0	1.1	.1	.5	17.8	17.3	1.3	1.6	.3
1956	39.9	39.9	—	1.8	1.8	—	.4	.4	—	1.1	1.2	.1	.4	19.5	19.1	1.3	1.6	.3
1957	42.6	42.6	—	1.9	1.9	—	.5	.5	—	1.1	1.1	*	.5	21.4	20.9	*	.4	.4

SOURCES: The federal breakdowns are based on estimates prepared by Mr. Samuel Cohn, Mrs. Naomi Sweeney, and Mr. Charles Stockman of the Bureau of the Budget. The series on state-local expenditures for 1952-1957 were constructed from data given in the annual *Summary of Governmental Finances*, Bureau of the Census; for earlier years the principal source is *Historical Statistics on State and Local Government Finances 1902-1953*, Bureau of the Census, Government Printing Office. The process involved extracting "assistance and subsidies" from Census data and recasting the resulting Census series into the Budget Bureau's functional classification scheme.

* Less than 50 million.

	(7)			(8)			(9)			(10)			(11)		
	Natural Resources			Commerce and Housing			General Government			Sum of Columns 1, 2, 4-9[b]			Major National Security Less Defense Support in 1957[f] Dollars MNS*[d]		
Year	Fed.	Total	S&L	Fed.	Total	S&L	Fed.	Total	S&L	Fed.	Total	S&L	Fed.	Total	S&L
1947	.5	n.a.	n.a.	.1	n.a.	n.a.	1.3	n.a.	n.a.	17.8	n.a.	n.a.	16.7	16.7	—
1948	.7	1.0	.3	.6	3.8	3.2	1.3	4.4	3.1	18.5	33.7	15.2	15.3	15.3	—
1949	1.0	n.a.	n.a.	.7	n.a.	n.a.	1.1	n.a.	n.a.	24.8	n.a.	n.a.	16.3	16.3	—
1950	1.2	1.6	.4	.6	4.9	4.3	1.2	4.7	3.5	23.6	43.1	19.5	16.2	16.2	—
1951	1.3	n.a.	n.a.	.7	n.a.	n.a.	1.3	n.a.	n.a.	29.4	n.a.	n.a.	26.2	26.2	—
1952	1.3	1.8	.5	.9	6.0	5.1	1.4	5.3	3.9	51.1	73.8	22.7	49.4	49.4	—
1953	1.4	1.8	.4	.9	6.8	5.9	1.4	5.5	4.1	58.8	83.6	24.8	55.5	55.5	—
1954	1.3	1.8	.5	.7	7.2	6.5	1.2	5.7	4.5	55.5	83.0	27.5	52.4	52.4	—
1955	1.2	1.7	.5	.6	7.9	7.3	1.1	5.9	4.8	47.6	77.9	30.3	43.8	43.8	—
1956	1.1	1.7	.6	.7	8.5	7.8	1.6	6.7	5.1	47.9	80.9	33.0	41.9	41.9	—
1957	1.3	1.9	.6	.7	9.5	8.8	1.7	7.4	5.7	49.8	86.2	36.4	42.6	42.6	—

[a] "Economic aid" is obtained by subtracting "defense support," "conduct of foreign affairs," and "foreign information and exchange activities" from Column 2. The figures for the latter two items are from Special Analysis L, *The Budget of the U.S.*, 1960.

[b] The figures do not agree with the series on G, FG, and SG as given in Table 1. The difference can be accounted for as follows: (1) The series in Table 1 excludes the value of government sales whereas the totals given here do not. (Since there is no published information on government sales by function, it is not possible to exclude such sales by functional categories); (2) The expenditure totals in the Cohn-Sweeney-Stockman table on which the federal functional breakdown is based differ somewhat from the official Commerce Department totals; (3) The Census Bureau figures which were used to provide the functional breakdown of state and local expenditure yield totals for SG which differ somewhat from the Commerce Department figures.

[d] Column 1 deflated by averaged quarterly index for FG, *U.S. Income and Output*, 1958.

TABLE 8 RELATION OF FUNCTIONAL COMPONENTS TO TOTAL ALL-GOVERNMENT, FEDERAL, AND STATE-LOCAL PURCHASES OF GOODS AND SERVICES, FISCAL 1947-1957[a]

(Per Cent)

Year	(1) Ratio of Own "Major National Security" Less Defense Support to			(2) Ratio of Own International Affairs Plus Defense Support to			(3) Ratio of Own Economic Aid to			(4) Ratio of Own Veterans' Services and Benefits to			(5) Ratio of Own Labor and Welfare to		
	FG	G	SG	FG	G	SG	FG	G	SG	FG	G	SG	FG	G	SG
1947	66.3	41.5[b]	—	11.8	7.4[b]	—	n.a.	n.a.	—	10.7	n.a.	n.a.	1.7	n.a.	n.a.
1948	60.5	33.2	—	13.0	7.1	—	n.a.	n.a.	—	8.1	4.5	n.a.	1.6	25.8	55.3
1949	50.8	30.6[b]	—	21.4	12.9[b]	—	n.a.	n.a.	—	6.0	n.a.	n.a.	1.2	n.a .	n.a.
1950	54.2	29.7	—	19.1	10.4	—	n.a.	n.a.	—	7.6	4.2	n.a.	1.7	26.7	56.9
1951	75.2	44.7[b]	—	11.9	7.1[b]	—	n.a.	n.a.	—	4.1	n.a.	n.a.	1.4	n.a.	n.a.
1952	85.1	58.9	—	4.7	3.3	—	.3	.2	—	2.7	2.0	.4	.8	17.9	56.4
1953	83.8	59.0	—	3.4	2.4	—	.4	.3	—	1.9	1.4	.4	.7	17.2	56.5
1954	83.2	55.7	—	2.9	1.9	—	.7	.5	—	2.0	1.4	.4	.7	19.3	56.7
1955	83.6	51.1	—	4.4	2.7	—	.8	.5	—	2.1	1.4	.3	1.1	22.8	57.1
1956	83.3	49.3	—	3.8	2.2	—	.8	.5	—	2.3	1.5	.3	.8	24.1	57.9
1957	85.5	49.4	—	3.8	2.2	—	1.0	.6	—	2.2	1.3	0	1.0	24.8	57.4

[a] Ratios are relative to totals given in Column 10, Table 7, except as indicated in note [b].

Year	(6) Ratio of Own Agriculture to			(7) Ratio of Own Natural Resources to			(8) Ratio of Own Commerce and Housing to			(9) Ratio of Own General Government to		
	FG	G	SG	FG	G	SG	FG	G	SG	FG	G	SG
1947	−1.1	n.a.	n.a.	2.8	n.a.	n.a.	.6	n.a.	n.a.	7.3	n.a.	n.a.
1948	2.7	2.1	1.3	3.8	3.0	2.0	3.2	11.3	21.0	7.0	13.0	20.4
1949	9.3	n.a.	n.a.	4.0	n.a.	n.a.	2.8	n.a.	n.a.	4.4	n.a.	n.a.
1950	4.7	3.0	1.0	5.1	3.7	2.1	2.5	11.4	22.1	5.1	10.9	17.9
1951	−3.7	n.a.	n.a.	4.4	n.a.	n.a.	2.4	n.a.	n.a.	4.4	n.a.	n.a.
1952	−.4	.1	1.3	2.5	2.4	2.2	1.8	8.1	22.5	2.7	7.2	17.2
1953	3.9	3.1	1.2	2.4	2.2	1.6	1.5	8.1	23.8	2.4	6.6	16.5
1954	5.4	4.0	1.1	2.3	2.2	1.8	1.3	8.8	23.6	2.2	6.8	16.4
1955	2.7	2.1	1.0	2.5	2.2	1.7	1.3	10.1	24.1	2.3	7.6	15.8
1956	2.7	2.0	.9	2.3	2.1	1.8	1.5	10.5	23.6	3.3	8.3	15.5
1957	0	.5	1.1	2.6	2.2	1.6	1.4	11.0	24.2	3.4	8.6	15.7

[b] Ratios are relative to totals as given in Column 2, Table 1.

TABLE 9 RELATION OF NONDEFENSE FUNCTIONAL COMPONENTS TO NONDEFENSE G, FG, AND SG, FISCAL 1947-1957[a]

(Per Cent)

	(1) Ratio of Own Veterans' Services and Benefits to Nondefense			(2) Ratio of Own Labor and Welfare to Nondefense			(3) Ratio of Own Agriculture to Nondefense			(4) Ratio of Own Natural Resources to Nondefense			(5) Ratio of Own Commerce and Housing to Nondenfense			(6) Ratio of Own General Government to Nondefense		
Year	FG	G	SG	FG	G	SG	FG	G	SG	FG	G	SG	FG	G	SG	FG	G	SG
1947	48.7	n.a.	n.a.	7.7	n.a.	n.a.	−5.1	n.a.	n.a.	12.8	n.a.	n.a.	2.6	n.a.	n.a.	33.3	n.a.	n.a.
1948	30.6	7.5	n.a.	6.1	43.3	55.3	10.2	3.5	1.3	14.3	5.0	2.0	12.2	18.9	21.0	26.5	21.9	20.4
1949	21.7	n.a.	n.a.	4.3	n.a.	n.a.	33.3	n.a.	n.a.	14.5	n.a.	n.a.	10.1	n.a.	n.a.	15.9	n.a.	n.a.
1950	28.6	7.0	n.a.	6.3	44.6	56.9	17.5	5.0	1.0	19.0	6.2	2.1	9.5	19.0	22.1	19.0	18.2	17.9
1951	31.6	n.a.	n.a.	10.5	n.a.	n.a.	−28.9	n.a.	n.a.	34.2	n.a.	n.a.	18.4	n.a.	n.a.	34.2	n.a.	n.a.
1952	26.9	5.4	.4	7.7	47.3	56.4	−3.8	.4	1.3	25.0	6.4	2.2	17.3	21.5	22.5	26.9	19.0	17.2
1953	14.7	3.7	.4	5.3	44.6	56.5	30.7	8.0	1.2	18.7	5.6	1.6	12.0	21.1	23.8	18.7	17.0	16.5
1954	14.3	3.4	.4	5.2	45.5	56.7	39.0	9.4	1.1	16.9	5.1	1.8	9.1	20.4	23.6	15.6	16.2	16.4
1955	17.5	3.1	.3	8.8	49.4	57.1	22.8	4.4	1.0	21.1	4.7	1.7	10.5	21.9	24.1	19.3	16.4	15.8
1956	17.7	3.1	.3	6.5	49.7	57.9	21.0	4.1	.9	17.7	4.3	1.8	11.3	21.7	23.6	25.8	17.1	15.5
1957	20.8	2.6	0	9.4	51.3	57.4	0	1.0	1.1	24.5	4.6	1.6	13.2	22.8	24.2	32.1	17.7	15.7

SOURCES: See Table 7.

[a] The denominators consist of the totals given in Column 10, Table 7 *less* "major national security" [1/7] and "international affairs and finance" [2/7].

TABLE 10 RELATION OF ALL-GOVERNMENT FUNCTIONAL COMPONENTS TO GROSS NATIONAL PRODUCT, FISCAL 1947-1957[a]

(Per Cent of GNP)

Year	(1) Ratio of Major National Security to GNP MNS/GNP	(2) Ratio of International Affairs Including Defense Support to GNP	(3) Ratio of Economic Aid to GNP	(4) Ratio of Veterans' Services to GNP[b]	(5) Ratio of Labor and Welfare to GNP	(6) Ratio of Agriculture to GNP	(7) Ratio of Natural Resources to GNP	(8) Ratio of Commerce and Housing to GNP	(9) Ratio of General Government to GNP
1947[f]	5.2	.9		.8					
1948[f]	4.5	1.0		.6	3.5	.3	.4	1.5	1.8
1949[f]	4.8	2.0		.6					
1950[f]	4.8	1.7		.7	4.3	.5	.6	1.9	1.8
1951[f]	7.1	1.1		.4					
1952[f]	12.8	.7	.05	.4	3.9	0	.5	1.8	1.6
1953[f]	13.7	.6	.07	.3	4.0	.7	.5	1.9	1.5
1954[f]	12.8	.4	.10	.3	4.4	.9	.5	2.0	1.6
1955[f]	10.5	.6	.10	.3	4.7	.4	.4	2.1	1.6
1956[f]	9.7	.4	.09	.3	4.8	.4	.4	2.1	1.6
1957[f]	9.8	.4	.12	.3	4.9	.1	.4	2.2	1.7

SOURCES: See Tables 1 and 7, and *Survey of Current Business*, July 1958.

[a] Since the functional components are all gross of sales, GNP, too, is taken *gross* of government sales.

[b] For 1947-1952 the numerator consists of federal expenditures on veterans' services. The state-local figures are not available—they are almost certainly negligible.

TABLE 11 RELATION OF NONDEFENSE FUNCTIONAL COMPONENTS (G) TO NONDEFENSE GNP, FISCAL 1947-1957[a]

(Per Cent of Nondefense GNP)

Year	(1) Ratio of Veterans' Services to Nondefense GNP	(2) Ratio of Labor and Welfare to Nondefense GNP	(3) Ratio of Agriculture to Nondefense GNP	(4) Ratio of Natural Resources to Nondefense GNP	(5) Ratio of Commerce and Housing to Nondefense GNP	(6) Ratio of General Government to Nondefense GNP
1947[f] n.a.						
1948[f]	.6	3.7	.3	.4	1.6	1.9
1949[f] n.a.						
1950[f]	.7	4.7	.5	.6	2.0	1.9
1951[f] n.a.						
1952[f]	.5	4.5	0	.6	2.0	1.8
1953[f]	.4	4.7	.8	.6	2.2	1.8
1954[f]	.4	5.1	1.0	.6	2.3	1.8
1955[f]	.3	5.3	.5	.5	2.3	1.8
1956[f]	.3	5.3	.4	.5	2.3	1.8
1957[f]	.3	5.5	.1	.5	2.5	1.9

SOURCES: See Tables 1, 4, and 7.

[a] Nondefense GNP is here taken gross of government nondefense sales. It is equal to GNP plus government sales less "total national security gross of sales." For explanation see note [a], Table 10.

TABLE 12 GOVERNMENT EXHAUSTIVE EXPENDITURE ON EDUCATION, FISCAL 1952-1957

Year	(1) Total Education (Billions of Dollars)	(2) Higher Education (Billions of Dollars)	(3) All Other (Billions of Dollars)	(4) Ratio of Total Education to G[a] (Per Cent)	(5) Ratio of Total Education to Nondefense G[a] (Per Cent)	(6) Ratio of Total Education to GNP[a] (Per Cent)	(7) Ratio of Total Education to Nondefense GNP[a] (Per Cent)
1952[f]	8.4	1.3	7.1	11.6	30.8	2.5	2.9
1953[f]	9.5	1.4	8.1	11.5	30.5	2.6	3.1
1954[f]	10.6	1.5	9.1	13.0	31.2	2.9	3.4
1955[f]	12.0	1.5	10.5	15.8	34.5	3.2	3.6
1956[f]	13.3	1.7	11.6	16.9	35.7	3.2	3.6
1957[f]	14.5	2.0	12.5	17.1	36.5	3.4	3.7

SOURCES: *Summary of Governmental Finances, 1952-1957* (Bureau of the Census). See also Tables 1 and 4.
[a] G, Nondefense G, GNP, and Nondefense GNP are all taken gross of sales (see note [a], Table 10).

TABLE 13 GOVERNMENT INVESTMENT, 1952-1957

Year	(1) All-Government Investment (Billions of Dollars)	(2) All-Government Purchases of Durable Equipment (Billions of Dollars)	(3) All-Government Construction (Billions of Dollars)	(4) State and Local Government Investment (Billions of Dollars)	(5) Federal Government Investment (Billions of Dollars)	(6) All-Government Investment as a Proportion of All-Government Purchases of Goods and Services (Per Cent)	(7) Federal Investment as a Proportion of Federal Purchases of Goods and Services (Per Cent)	(8) Government Nondefense Investment (Billions of Dollars)	(9) Federal Nondefense Investment (Billions of Dollars)	(10) Government Nondefense Investment as a Proportion of Nondefense G (Per Cent)	(11) Federal Nondefense Investment as a Proportion of Nondefense FG (Per Cent)
1952[r]	24.4	14.7	9.7	7.0	17.4	33.9	35.1	9.4	2.4	34.4	49.7
1953[r]	25.8	15.3	10.5	7.4	18.4	31.3	31.5	8.9	1.5	28.6	20.9
1954[r]	26.5	14.8	11.7	8.4	18.1	32.6	32.8	10.0	1.6	29.5	20.6
1955[r]	27.7	15.1	12.6	9.7	18.0	36.5	38.6	9.7	n.a.	27.9	n.a.
1956[r]	25.1	12.3	12.8	10.2	14.9	32.1	32.0	11.6	1.4	31.2	24.7
1957[r]	27.6	13.8	13.8	11.4	16.2	32.7	32.7	12.7	1.3	31.9	26.8

SOURCES: Estimates based on data in *Summary of Governmental Finances, 1952-1957* (Bureau of the Census) and Tables 1, 3, and 4.

TABLE 14 AN INTERNATIONAL COMPARISON

	(1) Government Purchases of Goods and Services as a Proportion of GNP (Per Cent) G/GNP	(2) Government Purchases of Goods and Services for Defense as a Proportion of GNP[a] (Per Cent)	(3) Government Nondefense Purchases of Goods and Services as a Proportion of GNP[a] (Per Cent)	(4) Government Nondefense Purchases of Goods and Services as a Proportion of Nondefense GNP[a] (Per Cent)	(5) Government Interest and Transfer Payments and Subsidies in Relation to GNP (Per Cent)	(6) Total Government Expenditure (E) in Relation to GNP (Per Cent)
United States (1957[f])	19.6	9.9	9.7	10.8	5.9	25.5
West Germany (1953)	19.3	4.9	14.3	15.1	11.5	30.8
Belgium (1952)	16.8	5.8	11.0	11.7	14.4	31.2
United Kingdom (1953)	22.9	9.9	13.1	14.5	12.8	35.7
Canada (1953)	18.2	8.5	9.7	10.6	8.4	26.6
Sweden (1952)	18.4	4.8	13.6	14.3	7.5	25.9
United States (1953)	23.1 (23.5)	13.4	9.7 (10.0)	11.2 (11.6)	4.8 (4.9)	27.4 (28.4)

SOURCES: All figures for other than the U.S., as also the parenthesized U.S. figures, are taken from *Trends in Economic Growth,* study prepared for the Joint Committee on the Economic Report by the Legislative Reference Service, Library of Congress, GPO 1955, Table 8, p. 280. Unparenthesized U.S. figures, which are based on the most recent revisions, are from *Survey of Current Business,* July 1958 and *U.S. Income and Output,* 1958.

[a] "Defense" here is based on the "national defense" category of the Department of Commerce and hence the U.S. ratios are not identical to the defense and nondefense ratios in Tables 4 and 5, which make use of the somewhat more inclusive "total national security" concept. (As in the case of the earlier ratios, the defense and nondefense figures here are adjusted to a net-of-sales basis. For the reasons and the method, see note [b], Table 4.)

Table 15 Personal Consumption, 1929-1957

Year	(1) Personal Consumption (Billions of Dollars) C	(2) Personal Consumption in Billions of 1957 Dollars[a] C*	(3) Per Capita Consumption in 1957 Dollars C*/P	(4) Per Household Consumption in 1957 Dollars C*/H	(5) Share of Consumption in GNP C/GNP	(6) Share of Consumption in Nondefense GNP C/GNP-TNS
1929	79.0	133.0	1,091	4,419	75.6	76.1
1930	71.0	124.9	1,014	4,082	77.9	
1931	61.3	120.9	974	3,900	80.4	
1932	49.3	110.0	882	3,503	84.3	
1933	46.4	107.5	855	3,391	82.9	
1934	51.9	113.1	894	3,534	79.9	
1935	56.3	120.2	944	3,710	77.6	
1936	62.6	132.3	1,032	4,034	75.7	
1937	67.3	137.2	1,064	4,145	74.1	
1938	64.6	134.6	1,036	4,018	75.8	
1939	67.6	142.6	1,088	n.a.	74.2	75.2
1940	71.9	150.1	1,136	4,301	71.4	73.1
1941	81.9	160.0	1,199	4,457	65.1	73.1
1942	89.7	156.5	1,160	4,299	56.4	81.8
1943	100.5	160.5	1,174	4,350	52.2	89.2
1944	109.8	166.2	1,200	4,480	52.0	88.6
1945	121.7	177.9	1,271	4,744	57.0	87.1
1946	147.1	199.6	1,412	5,223	69.8	76.6
1947[r]	157.9	201.8	1,413	5,161	70.6	75.4
1948[r]	172.6	205.2	1,411	5,042	69.9	73.8
1949[r]	180.3	208.5	1,409	4,952	68.9	74.1
1950[r]	185.0	217.6	1,445	5,002	70.1	75.1
1951[r]	205.4	228.1	1,490	5,103	66.2	72.0
1952[r]	213.6	228.3	1,465	5,018	63.1	72.7
1953[r]	227.8	239.8	1,514	5,179	63.3	73.8
1954[r]	234.2	243.9	1,514	5,200	64.7	74.5
1955[r]	246.4	255.5	1,558	5,345	65.3	73.2
1956[r]	264.2	271.6	1,628	5,566	64.5	71.7
1957[r]	276.9	276.9	1,631	5,593	64.1	71.5

SOURCE: *Survey of Current Business,* July 1958.

[a] For derivation of the implicit price deflator for consumption, see note *, Table 3. (The 1947[r] deflator was constructed as in Table 3, with one difference: the rate of extrapolation is taken from the consumer price index for "all items.")

Table 16 Investment, 1929-1957[a]

Year	(1) Gross Private Domestic Investment[a] (Billions of Dollars)	(2) Non-residential Con-struction (Billions of Dollars)	(3) Producers' Durable Equipment (Billions of Dollars)	(4) Producers' Fixed Investment (Sum of 2+3)[b] (Billions of Dollars)	(5) Residential (Nonfarm) Con-struction (Billions of Dollars)	(6) Gross Private Domestic Investment as a Proportion of GNP (Per Cent)
1929	16.2	5.1	5.9	10.9	3.6	15.5
1930	10.3	4.1	4.5	8.6	2.1	11.3
1931	5.5	2.4	2.8	5.2	1.6	7.2
1932	.9	1.3	1.6	2.8	.6	1.5
1933	1.4	.9	1.6	2.6	.5	2.5
1934	2.9	1.1	2.3	3.4	.6	4.5
1935	6.3	1.3	3.1	4.4	1.0	8.7
1936	8.4	1.7	4.2	5.9	1.6	10.2
1937	11.7	2.5	5.1	7.6	1.9	12.9
1938	6.7	2.0	3.6	5.6	2.0	7.9
1939	9.3	2.1	4.2	6.3	2.7	10.2
1940	13.2	2.5	5.5	8.0	3.0	13.1
1941	18.1	3.1	6.9	10.1	3.5	14.4
1942	9.9	2.0	4.3	6.3	1.7	6.2
1943	5.6	1.4	4.0	5.5	.9	2.9
1944	7.1	1.9	5.4	7.3	.8	3.4
1945	10.4	2.7	7.7	10.4	1.1	4.9
1946	28.1	6.2	10.7	17.0	4.8	13.3
(1947)[cal.]	(31.5)	(7.7)	(16.7)	(24.4)	(7.5)	(13.4)
1947[f]	30.1	7.1	14.6	21.7	5.9	13.5
1948[f]	37.3	8.5	17.7	26.2	9.4	15.1
1949[f]	39.2	9.5	18.8	28.4	9.5	15.0
1950[f]	37.8	9.3	16.7	26.0	11.6	14.3
1951[f]	57.8	11.3	20.9	32.3	14.1	18.6
1952[f]	51.3	12.7	21.9	34.5	12.2	15.2
1953[f]	51.7	13.1	21.3	34.4	13.5	14.4
1954[f]	47.5	14.1	21.7	35.8	14.0	13.1
1955[f]	55.8	15.1	20.8	35.9	17.6	14.7
1956[f]	67.2	17.3	25.6	42.8	18.2	16.4
1957[f]	67.5	18.8	28.1	46.9	17.3	15.6

SOURCES: *Survey of Current Business,* July 1958 and *Supplement,* 1949; *Survey of Governmental Finances,* 1952-1957; *U.S. Income and Output,* 1958.

[a] 1929-1947[cal.] stand for calendar years; 1947[f]-1957[f] for fiscal years.

[b] "Producers' Fixed Investment" is defined as private nonresidential con-

(7) Producers' Fixed Investment as a Proportion of GNP (Per Cent)	(8) Residential (Nonfarm) Construction as a Proportion of GNP (Per Cent)	(9) Producers' Fixed Investment as a Proportion of Nondefense GNP (Per Cent)	(10) Producers' Fixed Investment*[d] (Billions of 1957 Dollars)	(11) Public plus Private Fixed Investment as a Proportion of GNP[e] (Per Cent)	(12) Public plus Private Nondefense Fixed Investment as a Proportion of Nondefense GNP[f] (Per Cent)
10.5	3.4	10.5	26.5		
9.4	2.3		21.7		
6.8	2.1		14.1		
5.0	1.0		10.6		
4.5	.9		7.4		
5.2	.9		9.4		
6.1	1.4		11.8		
7.1	1.9		15.8		
8.4	2.1		18.9		
6.6	2.3		13.9		
6.9	3.0		15.8		
8.0	3.0		19.5		
7.9	2.8		22.7		
4.0	1.1		13.0		
2.8	.5		10.6		
3.5	.4		14.1		
4.9	.5		19.8		
8.0	2.3		29.2		
(10.4)	(3.2)	(11.0)	(36.1)		
9.7	2.6	10.4	34.5		
10.6	3.8	11.2	37.2		
10.8	3.6	11.6	37.3		
9.9	4.4	10.6	34.5		
10.4	4.5	11.3	39.4		
10.2	3.6	11.7	40.3	21.0	19.1
9.5	3.8	11.1	39.6	20.5	18.4
9.9	3.9	11.4	40.5	21.1	19.0
9.5	4.7	10.7	40.1	21.5	18.8
10.5	4.4	11.6	45.7	21.0	19.7
10.8	4.0	12.1	46.9	21.2	19.9

struction plus producers' durable equipment. (The components will not necessarily add to the total because of rounding.)

[d] The implicit price deflators for all but fiscal 1947 are those of the Department of Commerce (*U.S. Income and Output,* 1958). The figure for fiscal 1947 was derived as follows: By applying the rates of change, respectively,

of the Aberthaw Industrial Building Index (*Survey of Current Business, Supplement,* 1949, p. 36) and the U.S. Department of Labor Wholesale Price Index for "Metals and Metal Products" (*ibid.,* p. 30) to the Commerce Department's implicit price deflators for nonresidential construction and producers' durable equipment, both adjusted to a base of 1957[f]=100. The resultant deflators were used to deflate the raw figures for 1947[f] (Columns 2 and 3) and these were then added to yield producers' fixed investment for fiscal 1947 in 1957[f] dollars.

[e] "Public plus private fixed investment" equals "private fixed investment" (i.e., producers' fixed investment plus residential construction) plus all-government investment (as in Column 1, Table 13).

[f] Public nondefense investment is as in Column 8, Table 13. Private fixed investment is as defined in note [e] above. For the series on nondefense GNP, see Table 5.

[g] Includes net increases in business inventories.

INDEX

Other Books by Members of the
CENTER FOR INTERNATIONAL STUDIES,
MASSACHUSETTS INSTITUTE OF TECHNOLOGY
Published by Harper & Brothers

A Proposal: Key to an Effective Foreign Policy
by M. F. Millikan and W. W. Rostow, 1957

Forging a New Sword: A Study of the Department of Defense
by William R. Kintner, with Joseph I. Coffey and Raymond J. Albright, 1958

The American Style: Essays in Value and Performance
edited by Elting E. Morison, 1958

The United States in the World Arena: An Essay in Recent History
by W. W. Rostow, 1960

Postwar Economic Trends in the United States
edited by Ralph E. Freeman, 1960